# Metal
# Clay
# Origami
# Jewelry

# Metal
# Clay
# Origami
# Jewelry

## 25 CONTEMPORARY PROJECTS

Sara Jayne Cole

LARK
CRAFTS

A Division of Sterling Publishing Co., Inc.
New York / London

**EDITOR:** Linda Kopp

**ART DIRECTOR:** Kristi Pfeffer

**ART ASSISTANT:** Bradley Norris

**ILLUSTRATOR:** Orrin Lundgren

**PHOTOGRAPHER:** Stewart O'Shields

**COVER DESIGNER:** Celia Naranjo

Cole, Sara Jayne.
  Metal clay origami jewelry : 25 contemporary projects / Sara Jayne Cole. -- 1st ed.
      p. cm.
  Includes index.
  ISBN 978-1-60059-533-2 (pb-trade pbk. : alk. paper)
  1.  Origami. 2.  Precious metal clay. 3.  Jewelry making.  I. Title.
  TT870.C598 2010
  736'.982--dc22

                    2009046850

10 9 8 7 6 5 4 3 2 1

First Edition

Published by Lark Books, A Division of
Sterling Publishing Co., Inc.
387 Park Avenue South, New York, NY 10016

Text © 2010, Sara Jayne Cole
Photography © 2010, Lark Books, A Division of Sterling Publishing Co., Inc.
Illustrations © 2010, Lark Books, A Division of Sterling Publishing Co., Inc.

Distributed in Canada by Sterling Publishing,
c/o Canadian Manda Group, 165 Dufferin Street
Toronto, Ontario, Canada M6K 3H6

Distributed in the United Kingdom by GMC Distribution Services,
Castle Place, 166 High Street, Lewes, East Sussex, England BN7 1XU

Distributed in Australia by Capricorn Link (Australia) Pty Ltd.,
P.O. Box 704, Windsor, NSW 2756 Australia

If you have questions or comments about this book, please contact:
Lark Books
67 Broadway
Asheville, NC 28801
828-253-0467

Manufactured in China

ISBN 13: 978-1-60059-533-2

For information about custom editions, special sales, premium and corporate purchases, please contact Sterling Special Sales Department at 800-805-5489 or specialsales@sterlingpub.com.

For information about desk and examination copies available to college and university professors, requests must be submitted to academic@larkbooks.com. Our complete policy can be found at www.larkbooks.com.

# Contents

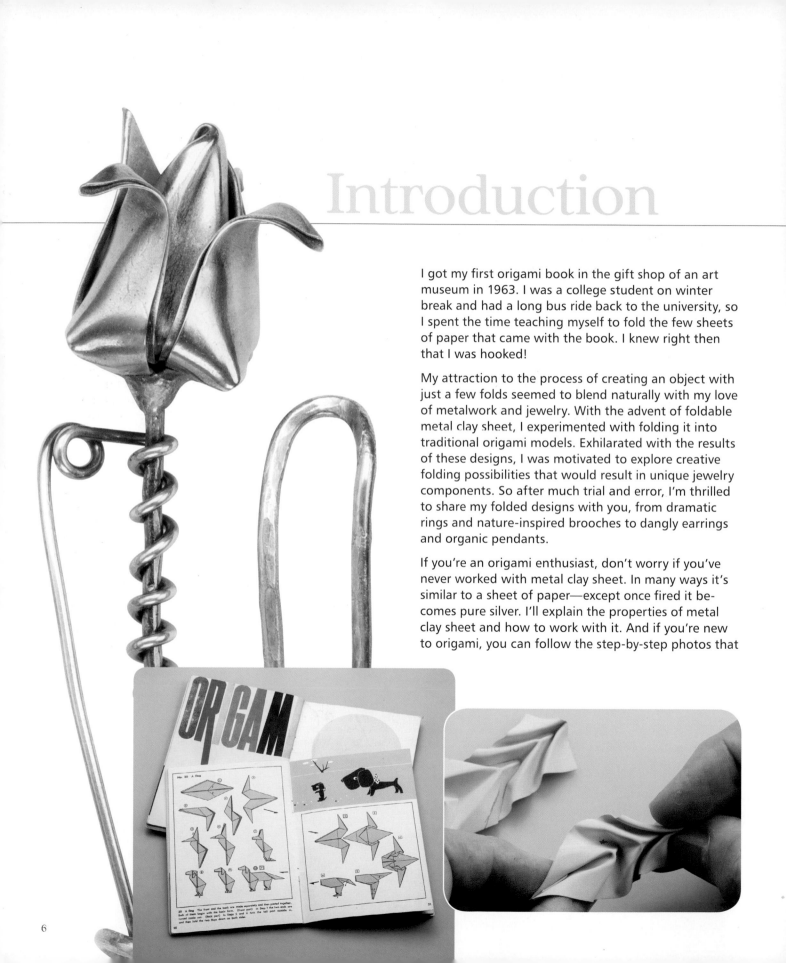

# Introduction

I got my first origami book in the gift shop of an art museum in 1963. I was a college student on winter break and had a long bus ride back to the university, so I spent the time teaching myself to fold the few sheets of paper that came with the book. I knew right then that I was hooked!

My attraction to the process of creating an object with just a few folds seemed to blend naturally with my love of metalwork and jewelry. With the advent of foldable metal clay sheet, I experimented with folding it into traditional origami models. Exhilarated with the results of these designs, I was motivated to explore creative folding possibilities that would result in unique jewelry components. So after much trial and error, I'm thrilled to share my folded designs with you, from dramatic rings and nature-inspired brooches to dangly earrings and organic pendants.

If you're an origami enthusiast, don't worry if you've never worked with metal clay sheet. In many ways it's similar to a sheet of paper—except once fired it becomes pure silver. I'll explain the properties of metal clay sheet and how to work with it. And if you're new to origami, you can follow the step-by-step photos that

accompany nearly every folding step. You'll start out learning a few basic origami terms and then move to folding origami bases which allows you to create the foundation of many of the projects. From there you're prepared to begin the projects. If you're new to folding you might want to start with Samurai Pin (112) or Winged Earrings (116). Once you're comfortable with the basic folds or if you're an accomplished folder, you're ready for a more challenging piece like First Origami Pendant (50) or Lily Pin (84).

With this book I can celebrate my excitement for both metal clay sheet and origami. I hope my designs will show you that with just a few folds you can make impressive silver jewelry. In addition, I've included some project variations showing how the addition of a stone, simple surface texture, or patina can dramatically change the appearance of a piece. I encourage you to experiment along the way and hope that you'll be inspired to experiment with folding and fashion your own origami creations—after all, that's how these designs came to be.

# About Origami

Creative origami from geometric to expressive is being made all over the world. Although origami looks complicated, making a figure with folds is easy to learn. All you need to start is a square piece of paper—or, in this case, metal clay sheet—and a hard surface to fold against. Careful, accurate creases together with the correct sequence of steps bring about a transformation of a flat sheet to a sculptural form.

## Origami Glossary

The terms below are universal to origami. While you'll be able to follow step-by-step photographs to create the projects, understanding this basic terminology will prove beneficial when reading the text accompanying the photos.

### VALLEY FOLD

Fold the paper/sheet forward onto itself. When unfolded, the crease forms a valley.

### MOUNTAIN FOLD

The folded edge goes behind itself and when unfolded leaves a ridge.

## words of advice

Origami is harder to explain than it is to do. Rely on the photos. Practice with a piece of paper. Do this! Keep in mind that metal clay is a lot more elastic than paper, even flimsy paper. Some projects will fold perfectly in paper. But some—the more fluid ones, like the Pocket Pendant—won't fold as well in paper because the paper is just too stiff. But still—do a trial run. Almost always, if you read an instruction that looks complicated, but then hold a piece of paper in your hand and try it, you'll say, "Oh, is THAT all?"

### SQUASH FOLD

After making a mountain or a valley fold, this fold is made by lifting a flap and opening the pocket. Then the flap is squashed down into a new position.

### INSIDE REVERSE FOLD

Tuck a flap inside by opening out a mountain fold and pushing down on the crease line so the fold reverses and is now inside.

## SINK FOLD

This advanced fold entails a closed point to be sunk inside the model.

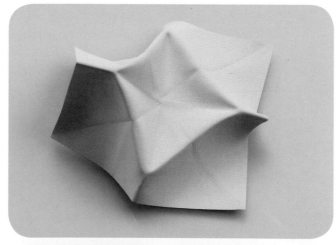

## Basic Origami Bases

Origami has some basic forms—called bases— that are achieved by creating a certain set of creases and folds in sequence. By learning these base folds, you'll know how to create the traditional origami models. Note that not all of the projects in this book start from a base.

Below are three base origami folds that can be folded with metal clay sheet. Before folding with metal clay sheet, I strongly recommend first practicing the folds using origami paper. Wait; let me repeat that for emphasis. Before folding with metal clay sheet, I highly advise you to practice the folds first using origami paper. Precut packs of multicolored origami paper are available in a variety of sizes at your local craft supply store or online. This paper is designed for origami so it's ideal for folding. One side has color while the other side is white. This helps when learning to sequence the origami fold.

**TIP:** If you don't have origami paper, cut a square from lightweight wrapping paper or printer paper. Measure and cut with care so you have an exact square. Most origami models start with a square but there are some that use a rectangle, hexagon, and circle.

Find yourself a workspace where you can lay out the instructions and have plenty of room to fold on a flat smooth surface.

### words of advice

Although these bases seem quite simple, with a few alterations, they can be used to create advanced and intricate pieces like this one. For more inspiration, see page 124.

## PRELIMINARY BASE

This is a series of four folds that are the beginning to many origami models. It's called the Preliminary Base in origami because other more advanced bases can be developed from it.

1. Begin with a perfect square.

2. Crease and unfold one diagonal.

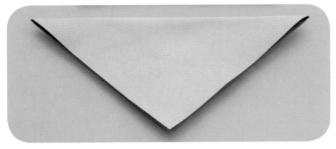

3. Fold the opened square in half toward you, forming a rectangle.

4. Bring the right corner over along the diagonal crease line so the right outside edge rests along the lower outside edge.

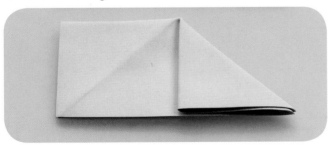

5. Repeat this step in reverse on the left side, folding the left top corner along the diagonal crease line on the backside of the rectangle.

6. The triangle that is formed has the long open edges facing you, and the top 90° angle is away from you.

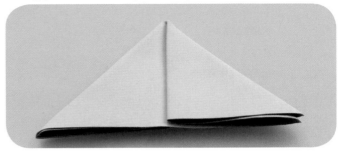

7. Place your thumbs in the pocket at the open edge and, holding the 45° angles, bring these together forming a diamond with the top enclosed and the bottom open.

**TIP:** When making the crease guideline folds, make sure the edges and corners line up before pressing the crease line. Always press the clay with your fingers—don't score the creases like you would with paper by using a fingernail or a folding tool. These might tear the clay sheet. Let the work surface be a tool for holding the clay sheet, and fold against it.

The one action that might be tricky is the last step when bringing the two outside angles to the center and turning the folded piece one-half turn to make a diamond with a smooth, flat, unbroken surface.

## FROG BASE

The Frog Base is a classic base that begins with the Preliminary Base. The Frog Base is the building fold sequence for the frog, lily, and other traditional origami models.

1. Begin with the Preliminary Base placed so the open edges are facing you.

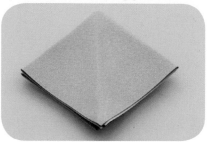

2. Lift one flap and open the pocket.

3. Push down, spread, and flatten the pocket.

4. Fold the lower flap over so its lower edge rests on the center.

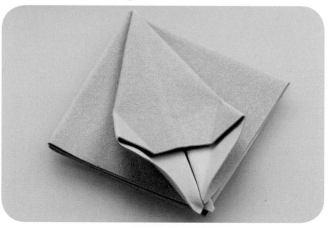

5. Unfold the last step.

6. Lift the center of the edge that was made in step 3.

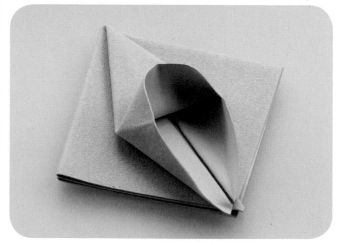

**7.** Fold this point up, pulling in the sides formed in step 4.

**8.** Fold the small top triangle down.

**9.** Repeat steps 2 through 8 on the remaining three flaps.

## WATERBOMB BASE

The Waterbomb Base is a traditional base formed by bringing the midpoints of the four edges of a square together, forming a pyramid. This pyramid is used in folding a traditional box that could be filled with water.

**1.** Fold the paper in half away from you, forming a rectangle. Unfold the rectangle so it lies flat.

**2.** Folding toward you, fold the paper in half, bringing the opposite corners together. You now have a triangle shape.

**3.** Unfold this triangle, and repeat the last fold using the other two corners.

**4.** Open out the sheet and lift the two outer edges of the horizontal crease fold. Bring those two points together in the center.

**5.** The diagonal crease lines will collapse over these two points as they meet, forming a pyramid.

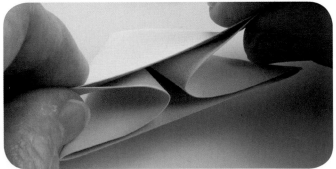

## THE PINWHEEL

While not a traditional base, the pinwheel is one of the best-known origami patterns of all time, beloved by school children playing with colored paper and restaurant patrons toying with cocktail napkins. I've made it dozens of times, and I kept asking, What if? What if I pulled this flap that way instead of the other way?

1. Make diagonal crease guidelines from corner to corner, and open the sheet out flat.

2. Fold the sheet exactly in half, making a center guideline, then open it back out flat.

3. Valley-fold each half to the center guideline.

4. With the open side facing up, mountain-fold the sheet in half, bringing the short ends together.

5. Valley-fold and unfold each end to the center fold, making guidelines for the next step.

6. Holding the corners of the top layer where they meet in the center, lift these two corners up and out. Fold along the diagonal creases and valley-fold the entire layer in half, along the guide creases you made in step 5. Each diagonal crease line becomes the center fold of a corner, making pointed "wings" on each side.

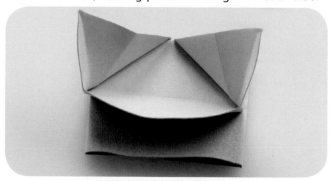

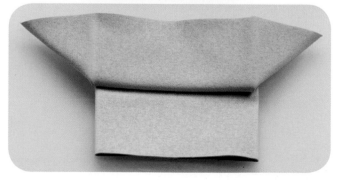

7. Turn the piece over and repeat the last step. At this point, the piece will resemble a boat.

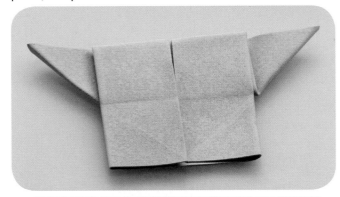

8. Open out the piece so the two open edges meet.

9. Fold over the top right flap to the right along the diagonal crease line. Repeat with the opposite flap to make a pinwheel.

# About Metal Clay Sheet

Origami was developed using paper for folding. Some adventurous folders began to use fabric while still others experimented with polymer clay, but because of its nature, folding metal remained out of the question. Now the innovation of the Japanese has given origami enthusiasts a way to fold metal—using metal clay sheet (also referred to as metal clay paper).

Artists can now use the same origami folding techniques traditionally used with paper to fold metal clay sheet. Once fired, the folded metal clay origami model emerges from the kiln as pure silver. It sounds quite magical, but metal clay's composition makes this process possible. Metal clay is made up of microscopic grains of pure metal held together by an organic binder and moisture. During firing, the binder burns away and the finished pure silver piece is 12 to 15 percent smaller. The Mitsubishi Corporation—under the brand name of PMC (Precious Metal Clay)—invented metal clay in the early 1990s, and other manufacturers followed suit. Aida Chemical Industries now produces Art Clay Silver (ACS). Both of these Japanese companies have since produced a paper-like metal clay. PMC sheet is available in sheets that are the thickness of a heavy paper and measure 6 x 6 cm. Art Clay Silver Paper is thicker and measures 75 x 75 mm.

## Metal Clay Sheet Properties

Metal clay sheet is a specially formulated material that has had its moisture content stabilized. This means that it's not subject to evaporation so it won't dry out and remains flexible until fired. The ability to fold and unfold this specially formulated material makes it ideal for origami. Folding metal clay sheet is like folding vinyl—a little bouncy, a little stretchy, and definitely floppy. Although you can fold metal clay sheet like paper, the material has its own unique texture and consistency, as well as advantages and limitations.

When making some traditional origami designs with paper, inside crease folds can be made by folding the entire piece of paper—in other words, the folding process creases all the layers. But because of the thickness of metal clay sheet, each layer will need to be folded individually. It might be necessary to leave off the final folding steps to avoid problems brought about by the sheet's thickness. Metal clay sheet has a stretchy quality that's good for lining up folds and for stretching folded pieces, lending an organic feel to the straight folds. Because metal clay sheet is made without water, the individual layers of the folded piece will remain separate after firing, allowing minor adjustments to be made.

Fired metal clay sheet is a thin 26-gauge fine silver that has little strength. When selecting a project, try to choose an origami design that folds back over itself, and don't leave any protruding single layers unsupported. Since the metal clay sheet is pure silver once fired, fragile areas can be reinforced using lump metal clay or traditional metalworking techniques. You can attach a fired piece of clay sheet to a heavier piece of metal by soldering or using cold connections.

# Supplies You'll Need

For the beginner projects in this book, you'll be using metal clay sheet and sterling silver wire with ready-made findings. I used the 2⅜-inch-square (6 cm) PMC sheet for the projects in this book; however, there is a rectangular size (1⅛ x 4¾ inches [2.6 x 12 cm]) that is good for projects that use quarter sheets.

**NOTE:** Unless otherwise specified, the projects in this book use one metal clay sheet. Projects that call for half or quarter sheets require you to cut a full sheet to the desired size. For easy cutting, leave the sheet in its plastic packaging, and use a metal ruler and utility knife to cut through both the plastic and the sheet.

## Basic Supply Kit

Besides your metal clay sheet, for any project in this book make sure you have the items on the following list.

Smooth, hard surface of nonstick silicone

Needle tool

Metal ruler

Utility knife

Kiln or butane torch

I can't overemphasize the importance of a smooth, hard work surface. This surface is your first folding tool. A sheet of smooth, nonstick silicone that can be cleaned between projects is good to cover your workspace. Any lint or grit on the work surface will be picked up in the metal sheet, leaving impressions on the unfired metal clay. When the clay shrinks during firing, those imperfections will really stand out.

**TIP:** If you work on a plastic or acrylic sheet, you can slide the piece off the sheet onto the kiln shelf later, without disturbing it.

The needle tool is a blunt needle on a wooden handle. It's useful for when your fingers won't fit into a tiny space. You'll need a utility knife and a metal ruler to ensure straight, accurate cuts.

## Additional Supplies Kit

The advanced projects will incorporate PMC+ in lump, slip, and syringe form as well as fine silver wire. In addition to the tools listed for the beginner projects, you'll need the tools listed below.

Reusable flexible nonstick sheet

Olive oil or olive-oil-based hand balm

Fine paintbrush

Distilled water

Rubber-tipped shaper

Salon file (fine)

Cotton swab

Wire cutters

Chain-nose pliers

Round-nose pliers

Round needle file

Cup warmer (optional)

# Attaching Findings, Other Types of Metal Clay, & Embellishments

After you have some experience working with folding metal clay sheet, you may choose to attach lump clay to the unfired origami piece. Items you may decide to attach include wire for beads, stones wrapped in metal clay, or a formed metal clay bail. All added metal clay will have to dry thoroughly before firing, but the metal clay sheet does not.

## Lump Metal Clay

Metal clay in lump form can be joined to metal clay sheet before the sheet is fired or after, with an additional firing. This lets the individual with no metal working experience make complicated multistep pieces. Developed before metal clay sheet, lump clay looks and performs much like a piece of potter's clay—it can be molded, carved, and stamped.

I can't stress enough that when using water to glue lump clay to sheet, use very little, as the unfired sheet will dissolve if it gets too wet. Because of that fact, I like to fire the metal clay sheet and then add clay and details in a second firing.

### ATTACHING TO UNFIRED SHEET

The lump metal clays that work best with sheet clay are the low-fire Art Clay 650, PMC+, and PMC3. These metal clays also come in slip and syringe forms that can help you produce an innovative piece of origami jewelry.

To keep the damp metal clay from sticking to you or your work surface, put some olive oil or a balm that contains olive oil on your hands and, if you don't have a nonstick sheet, a little on your work surface. When using metal clay in lump form, pinch off only as much as you'll need for the project. Keep the rest from drying out by returning it to the resealable package. Place the folded sheet on a nonstick surface so it won't need to be moved before the added lump clay is dry; this will avoid tearing or loosening the join.

1. Shape the lump clay into the piece to be attached.

2. Paint slip onto the area of lump clay that will be joined to the unfired clay sheet.

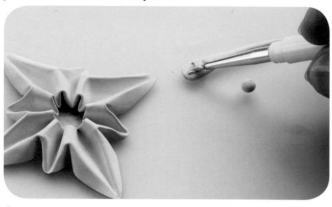

3. Make sure to support the joined area if needed until the lump clay is dry. Remember, the metal clay sheet will not dry out.

## ATTACHING TO A FIRED PIECE

Lump clay can be attached to fired sheet. Leave the white surface on the fired piece—don't clean or polish it. Remember that while the unfired metal clay will shrink 12 percent, the fired sheet has already reached its final size. To keep the fired shape from warping, use slip to attach the unfired clay to a small area of the fired piece.

1. Shape the lump clay as desired, use slip to attach it to the fired metal clay at the joint, and finish shaping the wet clay. To ensure a strong bond once fired, paint additional slip wherever the wet clay and fired clay touch.

2. If needed, support the joined area until the clay is dry, but be sure to remove the support before firing. The lump clay must be completely dry before firing.

## Findings

Findings are what are attached to the metal clay jewelry so it can be worn.

Using jump rings or wire-wrapping techniques, ready-made bails, ear wires, and ear posts can be attached through a hole made in the finished piece. You can drill a hole in the fired sheet using metalworking tools. Just be sure to position it away from the middle of a crease or from the edge; otherwise the hole may tear. Findings like one-piece pin clasps can be attached with epoxy.

## Attaching a One-Piece Pinback

Before mixing the epoxy, allow the metal clay piece to dry completely after tumbling, as fired metal clay is porous, and any moisture remaining in the tiny pores will keep the epoxy from bonding to the finding.

To ensure that your brooch sits nicely on fabric, position the pinback in the upper third of the piece. Before attaching, check to make sure the pin isn't visible from the front. Adhere the pin so the hinge is on the right-hand side and the clasp rotates down to close.

### ATTACHING FINE SILVER

Fine silver findings can be fired with the metal clay. To attach a fine silver finding to an unfired metal clay piece, paint a little slip on the area where you want to place the finding. Extrude a strip of syringe clay on top of the slip. Clean the finding with emery paper, paint it with a little slip, and place it on the extruded clay. Allow it to dry before moving it to the kiln shelf for firing. To attach a ready-made fine silver bail, brush a drop of very thick slip onto the unfired sheet where the bail is to be attached. Wrap the stem of the bail with lump clay, and place it in position. Do not move the piece until the lump clay is dry.

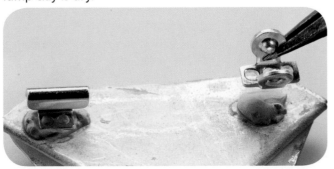

### USING STERLING SILVER

For ear wires that are incorporated into the design, make sure to attach an area—not just an end of the wire. I paint a thin slip of fine silver over the entire sterling wire so that the sterling doesn't turn black during firing.

**NOTE:** Findings can also be soldered to fired metal clay paper. However, if the finding will have stress on it, you must exercise care and solder it to all the layers of the sheet. Otherwise the stressed area may tear out over time. For items like pinback findings, solder the finding to a strip of sterling first, and then solder the sterling strip in place on the metal clay sheet.

## Making a Setting for a Stone

1. Rub a little olive oil on your hands, and get a pinch of high-density low-fire metal clay. This lump should be slightly larger than the stone. Form a ball in the palm of your hand and place it on an oiled surface, pressing down on the ball to flatten the sides but keeping it taller than the stone.

2. Use the point of a sharpened lead pencil to make an impression in the center of the clay. Place the stone in this indentation, and then press down on the stone's center until it sinks into the clay. Make sure a lip of clay appears around the top edge of the stone.

3 Determine where on your fired piece you wish to place the clay-wrapped stone. Use the slip brush, and paint a generous amount of slip on that spot. Paint a little slip on the bottom of the clay-wrapped stone, and place it in position.

4 After the added clay is completely dry, fire the piece at 1470°F (799°C) with a holding time of 30 minutes. To avoid shocking the stone, allow the kiln to cool to at least 300°F (149°C) before opening.

## Surface Embellishments

Embellishing options include attaching little scraps of sheet to the formed sheet, using syringe metal clay, or stamping the clay's surface.

Add decorative bits of unfired sheet by lightly brushing them with water and placing them on unfired sheet. Syringe clay is slightly thicker than metal clay slip and can be extruded onto unfired clay for some very nice decorative results. Stamping a pattern into unfired metal clay sheet is a simple way to add texture. Since the sheet is metal clay, it will hold a stamped pattern during folding, and, since the piece will shrink during firing, the stamped pattern will become more pronounced.

# Firing Metal Clay Sheet

Metal clay sheet has a firing schedule on the package with three choices of holding times and temperatures. The sheet has the same shrinkage rate as low-fired metal clay such as Art Clay Silver 650 or PMC+, which shrinks 12 percent.

It's important that your fired piece be properly sintered (where the metal has fused). An easy test to determine if sintering occurred is to place your folded, unfired piece on a sheet of paper and trace its exact outline. After the piece is fired, place it inside the tracing to check that it's smaller than the original outline. If the silver has sintered properly, the fired piece will have shrunk 10 percent.

One of the great things about metal clay sheet origami is that as soon as the folds are finished the piece can be fired. There's no drying time. The metal clay sheet remains in its flexible state, but because it is made without water, it's ready to fire immediately.

## Firing Options

Because I fire multiple pieces at one time, I use a programmable kiln to fire my work, but there are other satisfactory firing alternates available.

### PROGRAMMABLE KILNS

The easiest and most reliable way to fire metal clay sheet is in a programmable kiln. Once your pieces are placed inside you know that the temperature and timing are automatic no matter the size of the piece.

If you've worked with lump metal clay before and fired it in a kiln, you'll find that firing metal clay sheet is very similar. Sheet should be fired in a programmable kiln, which can hold the correct temperature for the precise length of time to ensure proper sintering of the metal. The kiln should be cold or if you have used it recently, allowed to cool to 300°F (149°C). You can place the folded piece directly on the removable kiln shelf to fire, but dimensional objects need support. For that I like to use "fiber blanket" that is made of non-asbestos fine alumina and silica threads bound together to form a cushion. The blanket provides protection along with support and can be torn or cut into pieces. Safe studio practices of wearing a mask while working with this fiber blanket are recommended.

Another handy item to have when firing is a metal container—I use a tuna can—full of vermiculite. Vermiculite pellets will cradle and support your origami piece during firing. Place the metal clay origami model in a shallow amount of vermiculite, and then pour more around it. Be sure to follow the manufacturer's safety recommendations when using vermiculite.

Set up a workstation close to your kiln that includes tongs and a heatproof surface. An insulated cookie sheet and a pair of long, stainless-steel barbeque tongs work fine. Use the tongs to remove the kiln shelf that holds your fired pieces, and set the shelf on the cookie sheet to cool. Although tempting, never touch the white fired metal clay until it's cool.

Each of the project instructions includes the recommended firing position and type of support for the best results. Because the layers of metal clay sheet will remain separate after firing, minor adjustments and repositioning can be made while finishing the piece, but try to position your piece well so you won't need to rely on this step. You can also change a design by lifting layers after the firing as part of your design concept.

## Kiln Firing Checklist

Programmable electric kiln

Fiber kiln shelf

Fiber blanket

Vermiculite

Small steel can (a tuna or cat food can works well)

Tongs

Insulated cookie sheet (or extra kiln shelf)

### OTHER KILN ALTERNATIVES

If you don't own a kiln and don't want to invest in a full-size kiln just now, you can contact your local bead shop or glass/enamel artisan. Many times they'll fire your pieces for a nominal fee. If you wish to fire on your own schedule, you might want to check out the Speed-fire Cone System (propane fired) or the Ultralite Kiln (a small 120V kiln). In comparison, they're relatively easy on the pocketbook. Using the manufacturer's directions, fire the projects in this book following the times and temperatures detailed in the project instructions.

### TORCH FIRING

This method takes concentration to be sure that sintering takes place and that you don't melt the thin sheet by overheating it. A butane torch is best for torch firing metal clay. They're lightweight and can be found in hardware stores or, since they're also used to caramelize sugar, on the shelves of cooking supply shops.

The most important point to keep in mind when torch firing is to make sure the clay sinters for the proper amount of time. Only pieces that are less than 2 inches (5 cm) around and weigh less than 25 grams should be fired with a torch. While you can fire your pieces longer than the recommended minimums, the silver will be brittle and will likely break if you don't fire your piece long enough.

**NOTE:** The Twin Pin, Eleanor's Star, and the Freeform projects in this book are all too large for torch firing.

## Torch Safety

When operating a torch, safety is paramount. Closely observe these rules:

• **Do not use supporting material like kiln blanket or vermiculite.**

• **Do not fire glass or pottery.**

• **Do not underfire by turning off the burner too soon.**

• **Do not touch the fired piece until it has cooled. The white color of the fired piece can fool you into thinking it's cool.**

### STEPS FOR TORCH FIRING

1. Set up your firing workstation in a well-ventilated place where the lights can be dimmed. Your work area must have a non-flammable surface that's at least 12 x 12 inches (30.5 x 30.5 cm); larger pieces of ceramic tile also work well. Place a firing brick or soldering block on the non-flammable surface. This is your firing surface.

2. Position the completed metal clay piece on the pad.

3. Turn on the torch and hold the torch at a 45° angle with the tip of the flame about ¾ inches (1.9 cm) from the piece. Sweep the flame in a slow circular motion to evenly heat the piece.

**4.** The first thing that happens is a sudden flame will play over the surface of the piece. Don't be alarmed: this is perfectly normal. The flame is burning off the binder material in the clay. It should last for a few seconds and then go out by itself.

**5.** Continue moving the torch slowly in a circular motion in order to heat the piece evenly. Concentrating the flame in one place will result in burning through the thin sheet. If you see a silver shimmer, back off the torch at once. Keep heating until the piece reaches a rosy orange color. When that color is reached, start the timer. This color is your heat indicator—try to keep the piece the same uniform orangey color for three to five minutes. Let cool completely before touching.

**NOTE:** When adding lump clay to a fired piece, allow the added clay to dry and torch fire it just as you did with the first firing, heating the entire piece evenly and holding the temperature for three minutes.

## Torch Firing Tool Kit

Butane torch

Non-flammable surface

Soldering pad, firebrick, or fiberboard

Tweezers

Timer

## Firing with Stones

Laboratory-created stones can be fired with metal clay if you slowly "ramp" (heat up) the temperature in your kiln. Your kiln instructions will tell you how to use the ramp speed feature. Refer to page 19 for how to create stone settings. Once the added clay is completely dry, fire at 1470°F (799°C) with a holding time of 30 minutes. After the firing is complete, allow the kiln to cool down slowly to about 300°F (149°C) before opening the door.

## Firing with Findings

Sterling silver findings can be fired in place when low-fire metal clay is used (see page 19 for how to attach findings). When firing an attached pin clasp and pin hinge, support the piece in vermiculite or cut a piece of fiber blanket to use as a support, so the piece can be fired faceup with the findings barely resting on the kiln shelf.

# Polishing Know How

When you take fired metal clay sheet out of the kiln, it has an amazing matte white color. This white is not a coating but the ends of tiny particles of silver that create what looks like an even surface. By burnishing this surface, the tiny points become compressed and smoothed out, causing the surface to become shiny silver. No matter the eventual finish I'm looking for, I always start by burnishing my pieces with a stainless-steel or brass wire brush and soapy water. You may decide that this satin finish is all the shine you want, but if not, you have some further options.

## Using a Tumbler

After I have brushed a shine on the piece, I put it in a tumbler along with stainless-steel shot and soap or burnishing compound mixed with water. This tumbling and burnishing helps make the soft fine silver stiffer by compressing the surface, which acts to harden the metal. Be sure you don't use abrasive media in the tumbler, because the surface of your piece will be worn away and the edges will disappear. I tumble my pieces about 20 minutes, choose the ones I want to oxidize (we'll discuss oxidation a little later on), and tumble the others for another 20 minutes.

## By Hand

Hand polishing with fine papers and polishing pads will achieve a similar result as tumbling, and no added equipment is needed. Polishing paper comes in different "grits"—the number of particles per square inch. For metal clay sheet, choose 600 grit or higher. This keeps the wearing away of the surface to a minimum. Begin rubbing your piece with a fine-grit paper and then proceed to an even finer grit. When using polishing paper or pads, always rub in the same direction. To finish off a hand-polished piece, you can shine up the highlights with a steel-burnishing tool and then buff it with a rouge polishing cloth. Rouge polishing cloths are actually two polishing cloths that are attached at one end. The inner cloth contains a compound that removes tarnish while the outer cloth is a soft flannel, perfect for a final polish. I don't like to use mechanical buffing wheels with sheet clay, because it can be too much too fast and, in the blink of an eye, your piece can be ruined.

## Choose a Path

Once you take your fired piece out of the kiln, you have a finishing decision to make—to patina or not to patina?

### FOR A SHINY SILVER FINISH

1. Burnish with a brass wire brush and soapy water.

2. Place in a tumbler with steel shot for 40 minutes, or hand polish. Check the progress after 20 minutes.

### FOR A PATINA FINISH

1. Burnish with a brass wire brush and soapy water.

2. Polish for 20 minutes in a tumbler with steel shot, or hand polish.

3. Oxidize with liver of sulfur solution.

4. More hand polishing or back into the tumbler for 20 minutes.

# Oxidation Patinas

A big part of what makes an origami piece so interesting are the folds and the crease lines. After a piece is fired, the resulting white and silver piece may appear soft and pleasing. To create a more dramatic presentation that brings out the folded details, use an oxidation solution. There are ready-made products that create oxidation, but my preference is liver of sulfur (LOS), the traditional product used to create the black antique oxidation that appears on silver naturally. It's best to work with LOS in a well-vented workspace.

**TIP:** Oxidize and polish your piece and any findings (wire, ear wires, bails, chains, etc.) at the same time so they'll match.

## Using Liver of Sulfur

To oxidize a piece using liver of sulfur, make a solution by combining a cup of warm water and a small lump of liver of sulfur in a small glass container. Wait for the sulfur lump to dissolve. When the liquid is pale amber yellow, use stainless steel tweezers to place your fired piece in the solution, and leave it until it's a uniform ash black. It's a good idea to oxidize any findings at the same time so they'll match the color of the finished piece. After the piece has become an ash black color, take it out of the solution and rinse thoroughly.

To accentuate the details of the piece, use fine pumice to rub the black off the high areas. Doing this will leave shiny silver highlights, while the black will remain in the recessed areas. Place your wet thumb in some pumice powder and a small amount will stick. With this pumice, use the soft pad of your thumb to rub the oxidation off the piece. This process creates a natural-looking shadow by leaving a feathered edge to the dark oxidation. Buff the piece by hand with a polishing pad, or place it in a tumbler to burnish it to a deep shiny silver and black.

## Achieving a Spectrum of Finish Colors

For some spontaneous fun, you can use liver of sulfur to finish your pieces in a variety of colors. You'll need two jars: one for the LOS solution and one for cold, clean water. The cold water will halt the color change, allowing you to inspect the piece to see if it's reached the color you want. It's important to throw out the clean water when it begins to look milky. Since heat speeds up the color changing process, you may choose to start with warm water, place your liver of sulfur solution on a cup warmer, or warm up the piece you wish to color.

To achieve an array of colors varying from yellow to red to blue, tumble your piece to a very high shine before dipping it into the LOS. Then, gripping the piece with stainless-steel tweezers, dip it in the LOS for a few seconds and then into the cold water to halt the color change. The piece will turn yellow, then proceed to a pale red, and finally to blue.

For even more variation, try adding ammonia (one tablespoon per cup of LOS solution) to the LOS solution to create an iridescent effect. Although it's hard to control the colors achieved with this method, unexpected results can add to the creative fun.

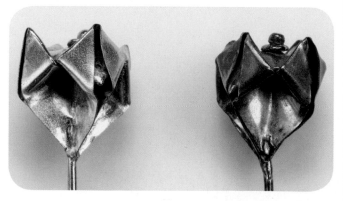

Another way to have varied colors on the same piece is to hold the tumbled piece in the LOS until it turns a uniform yellow. Rinse and dry the piece, and paint warm LOS on the areas where you want more color. After you see the color you like, let your piece sit in cold water that has had a little baking soda added to it. Rinse the piece thoroughly with soapy water.

Your desired color must be stabilized or the silver piece will carry on the natural process of oxidation and continue to turn darker. Spray the piece with an acrylic fixative—the kind artists use to seal their charcoal drawings. The satin finish spray seals the silver and keeps air out, thus halting the oxidation process.

## Supplies for Oxidizing with Liver of Sulfur

Liver of sulfur

Water

2 glass containers (custard cups or glass jars work nicely)

Plastic spoon

Stainless-steel tweezers

Ammonia (optional)

Soapy water

Paper towels

Baking soda

Pumice powder

Acrylic fixative

# The Projects

# Diagonal Fold Ring

One of the joys of metal clay origami is that the reverse side of a piece is often as appealing as the front. After designing and folding this ring, I discovered that I liked the back of it just as well. My original design is the project; the back is the variation.

## Materials & Supplies

Basic supply kit,
page 16

Additional supplies
kit, page 17

Supplies for oxidizing,
page 24

Plastic roller and
playing cards

**FOR THE RING**

Lump metal clay

Ring mandrel

Metal clay slip

**FOR THE VARIATION**

.999 silver ring band

½ inch (1.3 cm) of
16-gauge, round,
sterling silver wire

Half-drilled pearl

**TIP:** If you practice these folds first in paper—and surely you will—a glue stick or some very small paper clips will come in handy.

1. Using a soft lead pencil and a ruler, draw a diagonal line between two opposite corners of the sheet. This is just the centerline; it will not be folded. Don't press hard with the pencil when drawing the lines, to avoid tearing the metal clay sheet.

2. On each side of the centerline, draw seven lines parallel to it. The first should be ⅛ inch (3 mm) from the centerline; the rest should be ¼ inch (6 mm) apart.

3. Make the first folds along the lines on either side of the centerline. Mountain-fold these two lines, then valley-fold the adjacent lines, creating a diagonal center pleat.

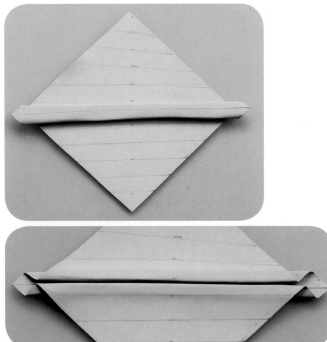

4. Completing one side at a time, alternate mountain and valley folds along the drawn lines. Make the valley fold a little before the drawn line, so the folded edges fall alongside each other; they should point in the same direction as the folded edges of the first pleat. Press these folds against the work surface with your fingers, to make them stay in place.

5. Fold the other side of the sheet as in step 4, making sure the folded edges point away from the center.

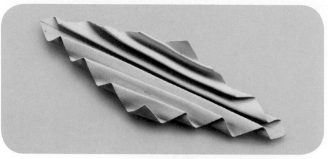

6. Fold the piece in half end to end, with the pleat on the outside and the longest points meeting. Press this halfway fold.

7. Make two more folds on each side of the halfway fold, folding each side back up and down again. The folds should decrease in height on each side of the halfway fold. There should be a total of five folded edges.

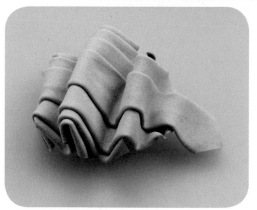

8. Stand the piece up. Holding the outer edges of the center group of pleats, tug out and down, so that the pleats also curve out and down, in telescope fashion. Repeat for the other four groups of pleats.

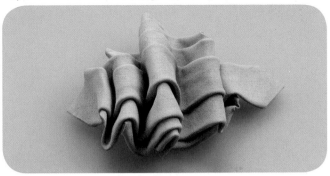

9. To make a ring band, roll a log of lump metal clay about four cards thick, and trim the edges to the desired width. Wrap this strip onto a ring mandrel two sizes larger than you want the finished ring to be. Trim off the excess ends at an angle, and seal the joint with slip.

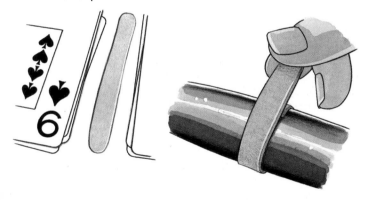

10. To create a round platform for the folded piece, roll a pinch of clay into a ball, then roll it to four cards thick. Trim out the width of the band from the circle and place the half-moon shapes on each side of the band.

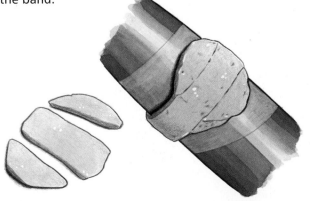

11. Allow the ring band to dry, then file any rough edges. Attach the folded piece to the finished band with slip.

12. Fire the ring on the kiln shelf, and add a patina to highlight the many folds.

**Variation**

For this variation, attach the origami shape backside-up to a .999 silver band, using metal clay and metal clay slip. If you plan to add a half-drilled pearl, attach the silver wire to the center of the origami shape before firing, using a little lump metal clay. The wire will serve as a post for the pearl. After firing is complete, trim the post to the right length, and attach the pearl.

# Fan-Fold Pendant and Earrings

This pendant-and-earrings set uses the classic back-and-forth fold that you've probably used to make a fan. With two distinct areas— a relatively smooth pyramid and a pleated base—the jewelry lends itself to two contrasting patinas. I added texture with fine plastic mesh and with appliquéd bits of metal clay sheet.

## Materials & Supplies

Basic supply kit,
page 16

Additional supplies
kit, page 17

Supplies for oxidizing,
page 24

Fine plastic mesh

8 inches (20.3 cm)
of 18-gauge, round,
sterling silver wire

1. First make a rectangle by cutting a strip ⅜ inch (1 cm) wide from one side of the sheet. Save this strip; you'll use it later.

2. Mountain-fold and unfold the rectangle in half end to end and side to side, to locate the midpoints. Texture half the sheet by laying plastic mesh over the surface and rubbing with a metal burnishing tool. Be gentle! The clay sheet is easy to distort or tear.

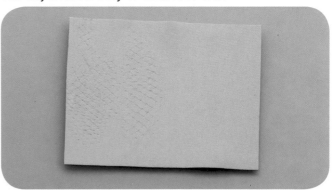

3. Fold the textured half into an arrowhead shape by folding under the textured sheet between the midpoint of the end and the midpoint of each side.

4. Measuring from the bottom of the rectangle, mark off three points on each side at $\frac{3}{8}$-inch (1 cm) intervals. Fold up the raw end at the first mark, then make two more folds straight across the rectangle in fan-fold fashion.

5. Retrieve the strip from step 1 and fold it in half, long sides together.

6. Now fold the piece along the centerline from the tip of the arrowhead to the fan fold. As you do, fold the fan in half and tuck it into the base of the arrowhead.

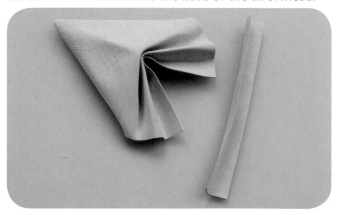

7. With its folded edge down, fit the extra strip into the center of the fan. With a little water and a fine-tipped brush, dampen the top edge of the strip where you want to join the two pieces.

8. Smooth the two edges together, and allow them to dry.

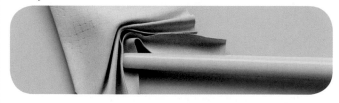

9. Trim the ends of the strip to match the existing fan, and save the trimmings.

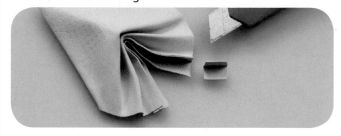

10. You need to ensure that the entire back of the pendant is flat and level—top to bottom and side to side—so it will lie comfortably on the chest when worn. Place the piece on the work surface, and hold the fan closed in the center. At the same time, lift up on the center of the arrowhead and push down on the center of the fan. Check that the back is flat and even.

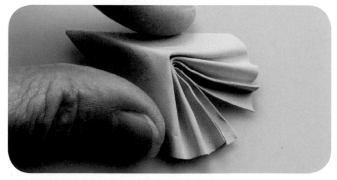

11. Seal the fan closed with a little water.

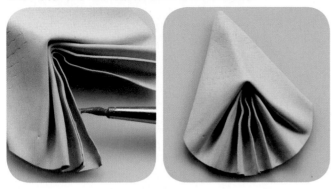

12. Trim excess clay off the back flaps, and seal the back closed with a little water brushed on one surface. Be sure to leave a good gap at the top point.

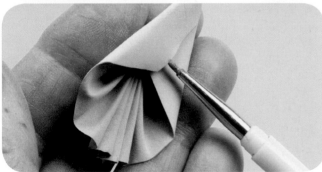

13. Cut the trimmings into triangles, moisten them, and position them randomly on the piece.

14. Fire the piece on the kiln shelf.

15. To make the bail, bring the ends of the sterling silver wire together and thread the ends through the hole in the top.

16. Pull the wire snugly up toward the tip. (You may choose to bend the center of the wire so it matches the angle of the back.)

17. Using the round-nose pliers, make a loop in both wires where they emerge from the tip, then wrap them around themselves. I chose a double-wire bail to balance the visual bulk of the piece.

18. The pendant is now ready to patina. See steps 13 and 14 of the Fan-Fold Earrings, page 36.

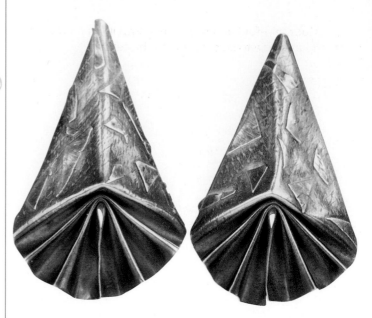

## Materials & Supplies

Basic supply kit,
page 16

Additional supplies
kit, page 17

Supplies for oxidizing,
page 24

Fine plastic mesh

Ear posts

Epoxy

1. Cut the metal clay sheet in half. Each half will become an earring and will follow the steps below.

2. Texture half the sheet by laying a piece of plastic mesh on the surface and rubbing with a metal burnisher. Be gentle! It's easy to tear or distort the clay sheet.

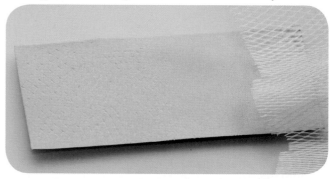

3. Mountain-fold and unfold the strip in half, both end to end and side to side, to locate the center.

4. Fold the textured half into a triangle by folding under the sheet between the midpoint of the end and the midpoints of the sides.

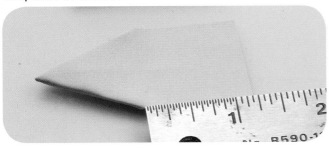

5. Measuring from the bottom of the rectangle, mark off five points on each side at ¼-inch (6 mm) intervals. Fold up the raw end at the first mark, then make four more folds straight across the rectangle in fan-fold fashion. You'll make five actual folds.

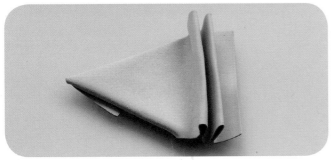

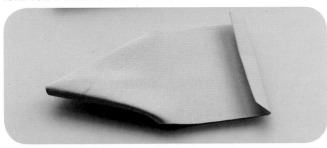

6. Fold the textured triangle in half. At the same time, fold the fan in half so it is tucked into the base of the triangle.

**NOTE:** Folding the fan in half makes the piece narrower and more three-dimensional, resembling an arrowhead. The sides of the triangle will slant downward, the fold in the center of the triangle will become more of a ridge, and a hollow cavity will form inside the piece.

7. Place the folded piece on the work surface, and nudge the triangle into a hollow shape, if necessary.

8. Now connect the fan where the two edges meet in the center. With a fine paintbrush, carefully brush distilled water on one end of the fan. Hold the two ends together until they are dry and will stay shut.

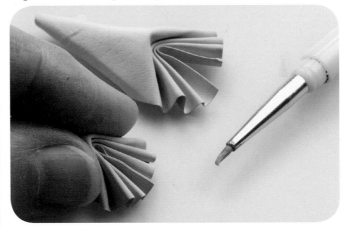

9. Trim off the extra metal clay that extends beyond the top of the triangle. Unfold the back of the triangle, and trim off that excess also.

10. Seal the back of the piece with water.

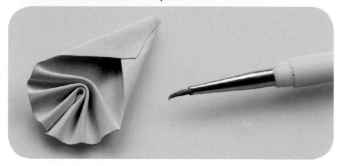

11. To add more texture, cut the four pieces of scrap into fragments. Using tweezers and a wet brush, dampen the fragments and place them at random on the textured triangle. Remember that water will dissolve metal clay sheet, so use less than you think you should!

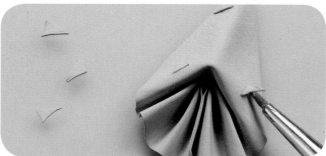

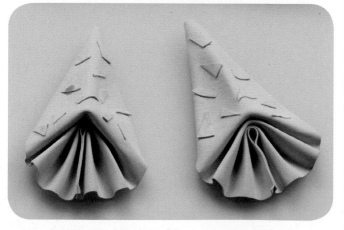

12. Fire the earrings flat on the kiln shelf.

13. To create an iridescent finish, use a solution of liver of sulfur and ammonia (see Achieving a Spectrum of Colors, page 24). To begin, dip only the fan end in the solution. Without rinsing, place the earring in a dish, and watch the colors change. It will first turn yellow, then darken to an iridescent copper. When you have as much color as you want, plunge the earring into cold water to stop any further change.

14. Now dip the entire earring into the solution, remove it, and set it on the dish. When you have the color you want, run fresh, cold water over the entire earring and allow it to dry.

15. Attach the ear post with epoxy. You can also create hanging earrings, using the same wire wrap that is used for the pendant (see page 33).

**TIP:** Patina both earrings and the Fan-Fold Pendant at the same time, and in the same solution, if you want them all to match.

You can vary the patina any number of ways. For example, you can patina only the fan end, stopping the process at its early, yellow stage, creating a lovely contrast in silver and gold.

# Eleanor's Star

This star evolved from my fascination with crease patterns. I love to unfold an origami sheet and admire the complex pattern of lines that results from even a few folds. I named the star for my mother, since I designed it on Mother's Day.

## Materials & Supplies

Basic supply kit,
page 16

Additional supplies
kit, page 17

Silver bail with post

Lump metal clay

Metal clay slip

10 to 14 mm dichroic
glass cabochon

1. Fold the Frog Base (see page 12).

2. Position the base so that the small triangle in the middle is folded down and the closed end points away from you.

3. Fold the closed top point so that it touches the tip of the small triangle flap. Press firmly to define the crease, and unfold.

4. Make this same crease fold on the other three sides with flaps. You need to fold this bulk over on all four sides to make sure an impression is made through the thickness of the sheet.

5. Open the folded sheet to see the crease lines, with the side facing up as shown.

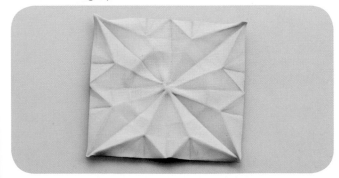

6. Pinch up the crease lines on the octagon in the center, making them all mountain folds. Sink-fold the octagon.

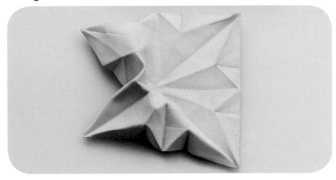

7. Now refold the Frog Base, following the original crease lines and beginning with the inner part of the base. Mountain-fold the creases that radiate from each corner of the octagon, and valley-fold the creases that radiate from the center of each side of the octagon. (Don't worry about grouping the creases in the sunken center; they'll be flattened later.)

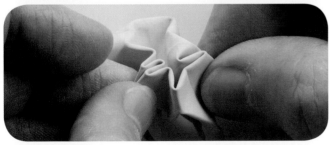

8. Now refold the outer edges of the Frog Base back into their original position. Lay the piece on the work surface, and remake the folds that are creased in the sheet, folding them inside, as shown. Lay the folded piece flat on the work surface, and press it firmly.

9. Stand the folded shape with the four points up, and open the points out slowly, pressing on the center balloon made by the sink fold.

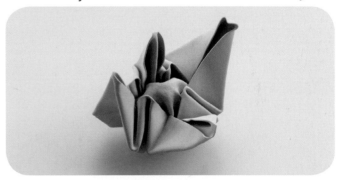

**10.** Turn the piece over and bring the center creases together, almost closing the center hole.

**11.** Take another look at the back, to make sure the balloon has collapsed into a neat circle.

**12.** Place the star on the work surface faceup, and pinch the tips of all eight points so they are well creased.

**13.** Arrange the points. Using a small-tipped clay shaper, bring out the sides of the four larger star points.

**14.** Now to attach the bail to the back of one long point. Roll a small ball of clay, and insert the post of the bail into it. Using the clay shaping tool, make a wedge-shaped indentation in the ball, so it will fit over the ridge on the back of the pendant. (Note: Be sure to position the indentation so that the opening in the bail will be parallel to the pendant.) Paint the assembled bail with slip and press it onto the star, low enough that it won't show from the front. Smooth the top slightly with the shaping tool. Set this aside, and do not move it until it's dry.

**15.** Tuck the cabochon into the center pocket. When the clay sheet shrinks during firing, the folds that form the pocket should touch it ever so slightly, holding it in place.

**Variation**

This version is very similar to Eleanor's Star except I left off the cabochon and oxidized the finish with a liver of sulfur solution. If desired, you could use an epoxy to attach a focal stone or cabochon after firing.

**16.** Slide the star onto the kiln shelf, give the points a final tweak if necessary, and fire it. (See Firing with Glass, below.)

**17.** Tumble the piece until the silver's brilliant shine complements the glittering glass cabochon.

# Firing with Glass

Firing with glass can be tricky. If the situation allows, I attach cabochons with epoxy after all the firings are complete. Because in Eleanor's Star the glass cab is tucked into a pocket, that wasn't an option, but I designed the piece so it requires only one firing.

To fire Eleanor's Star, bring the temperature up slowly at 500°F (260°C) per hour and hold at 1470°F (799°C) for 30 minutes. Cool the glass in phases as outlined at right.

**1.** When the 30 minutes are up, open the kiln and cool until the pyrometer reads 850°F (454°C).

**2.** Close the kiln door and watch that the temperature doesn't go back up past 1000°F (538°C). If it does, open the kiln and cool it down again.

**3.** Once the temperature remains below 1000°F (538°C), it's imperative to leave the kiln closed and to let it cool until it reaches room temperature.

While this process may take a while, it guarantees the surface of the glass will be shiny.

# Bulb Bead

For a new charm bracelet, I wanted beads sturdy enough to withstand lots of wrist action. After many crumpled balls of paper, I finally found my template for a rounded, hollow Bulb Bead. The bracelet pictured has beads in three sizes, all folded the same way.

## Materials & Supplies

### FOR THE LARGE BEAD:
full sheet of metal clay

### FOR THE MEDIUM BEAD:
2-inch (5 cm) square (trim half an inch [1.3 cm] off two sides)

### FOR THE SMALL BEAD:
quarter sheet

Basic supply kit, page 16

Additional supplies kit, page 17

Supplies for oxidizing, page 24

### FOR THE VARIATION
Fine plastic mesh

### FOR THE BRACELET
2-inch (5 cm) 18-gauge sterling silver head pin for each bead

Sterling silver chain bracelet with toggle clasp

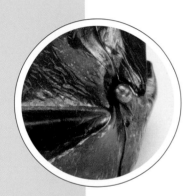

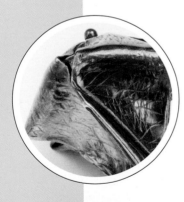

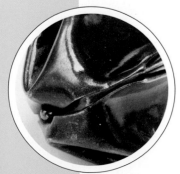

**NOTE:** To practice folding this bead, use thin, flexible paper, such as wrapping or origami paper. Just know that your trial bead won't be as satisfyingly round in any paper as it will become in malleable metal clay.

1. Valley-fold and unfold the sheet in half, making sure the corners match.

2. Fold the side edges to the center crease.

3. Working with only the top layer, valley-fold a triangular flap on each corner, bringing the top edge to the folded side edge; define the crease. Tuck the flaps inside with a mountain fold, and crease again.

4. Fold this long rectangle in half by folding the top forward, so the folds from step 3 are inside.

5. At the halfway fold from step 4, valley-fold one corner down, making a triangular flap. Do not bring the top, folded edge all the way to the center crease; rather, stop about ⅛ inch (3 mm) short of the center crease. Make a similar flap on the other side. Fold the flaps to both front and back, to make well-defined creases. These creases will be used later to make reverse folds.

6. Open the folded piece so it is once again a long rectangle with the tucked corners visible.

7. Fold up the right bottom corner so that the bottom edge falls just short of the left side of the piece; crease well. Repeat for the bottom left corner. Check these new creases; they should fall just inside the triangular flaps from step 3.

8. Repeat step 7 at the other end of the rectangle. The creases in steps 7 and 8 will be used to make reverse folds.

9. By lifting and folding, make a reverse fold in both layers of each center triangle. The diagonal creases that form the sides of the triangle will become mountain folds; the crease down the center of the triangle will become a valley fold.

10. Make a reverse fold in the single-layer triangle on each end of the piece.

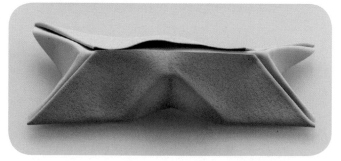

**11.** Paint distilled water very sparingly inside one single-layer reverse fold, and hold it shut until it stays that way. Repeat on the single-layer reverse fold at the other end.

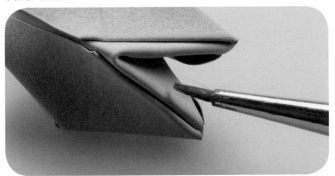

**12.** Now bring the tips together, watching that the two reverse folds in the center fall inside but do not close. An oval teardrop shape will form. You want to retain that rounded, hollow shape, so don't press too hard while joining the points, and don't press the bulb flat.

**13.** To make the sides stay together, paint a little water along one edge of the sides that meet above the middle reverse fold. Hold these sides together until they stay in place. (Don't pinch the very top closed. You'll need a small hole for the bead.)

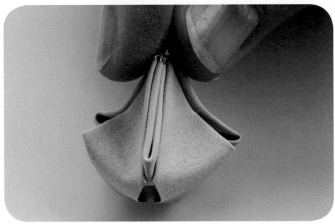

**14.** Check to make sure the bead has a hole in the top, and make one in the bottom with a needle tool.

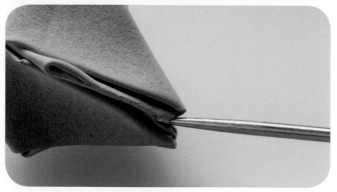

**15.** To fire the bead, stand it on its base in a nest of kiln fiber blanket. After the bead is fired, you may need to redefine the hole in the base.

**16.** Finish as desired. The beads shown were given an iridescent finish with a liver of sulfur and ammonia solution. (See Achieving a Spectrum of Finish Colors, page 24.) Patina the findings at the same time—before assembling the bracelet—for continuity of color.

**17.** To make the bracelet, thread each bead onto a head pin. Loop the pointed end through a link of the bracelet, wrap the wire around itself, and trim off the excess. To add interest, hang the beads at different lengths.

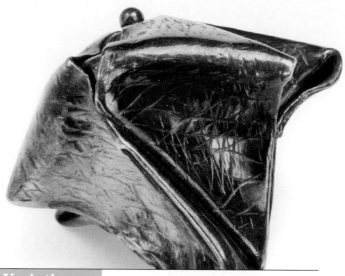

## Variation

To add texture to the bead, lay a piece of fine plastic mesh on the flat sheet of metal clay before you make your first fold, and rub the surface with a metal burnisher. Be gentle. The clay sheet is easy to tear or distort. Because the metal clay shrinks when fired, the texture will stand out on the finished bead.

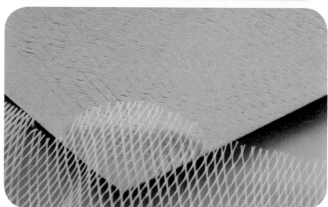

**TIP:** If you plan to tumble this bead with steel shot as part of the finishing process, put a pipe cleaner in the teardrop-shaped hole on the side, to keep the bead from filling up with shot.

# Butterfly Pin

Origami is full of patterns inspired by nature, including dozens of different butterflies. This version takes advantage of the thickness of folded metal clay sheet to hint at a body and head. For this colorful insect, I've added an iridescent patina to the finished pin.

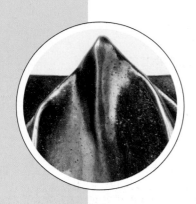

## Materials & Supplies

Basic supply kit, page 16

Supplies for oxidizing,
page 24

One-piece pin finding

Epoxy

Butterfly Pin

1. Begin by folding a Waterbomb Base (page 13).

2. Turn the base so that the top of the pyramid is facing toward you.

3. Fold the top two flaps down to meet in the center.

4. Turn the model over, and fold up all the layers so
that the tip extends beyond the top edge. Resist pressing down on this thick fold until you have completed
the next step.

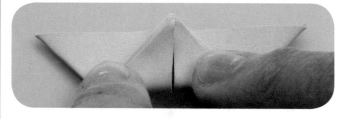

5. Fold down the two front flaps; this action will pull in their outer corners.

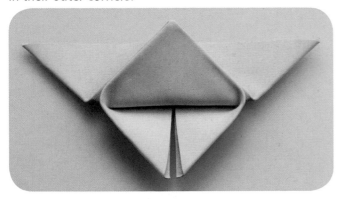

6. Exaggerate this small pocket by pushing in on the corner.

7. Now gently press down all the folds.

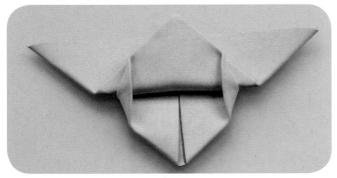

8. Suggest a head and body shape by pinching up the top center between the wings.

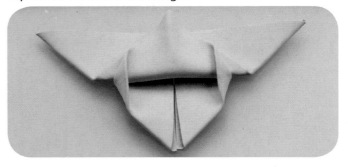

9. Fire the butterfly directly on the kiln shelf.

10. Brush the piece to a shine with a brass wire brush, then give it an iridescent patina with a liver-of-sulfur and ammonia solution.

11. Attach a one-piece pin finding with epoxy (see page 19 for attaching tips).

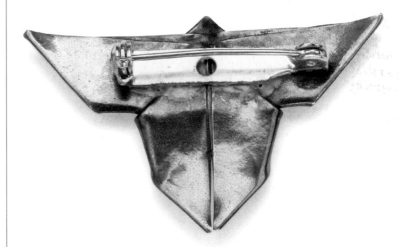

# First Origami Pendant

The first step for many origami projects (and for many origami bases) is to make a Preliminary Base. It is the most basic of bases. This handsome pendant is essentially a Preliminary Base with a few extra folds. Although it looks good dangling from a silver chain, you can give it a different look by wire-wrapping it to a decorative cord.

## Materials & Supplies

Basic supply kit, page 16

Additional supplies kit, page 17

Supplies for oxidizing, page 24

5-inch (12.7 cm) length of 20-gauge, round, sterling silver wire

Decorative cord

1. Make a Preliminary Base (page 11), and position it with the open end away from you.

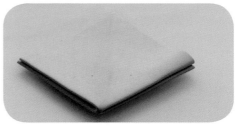

2. Fold the left top flap over so the open edge follows the center crease. Unfold, leaving a crease.

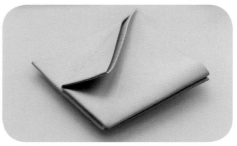

3. Fold and unfold the right open edge to the crease line made in step 2.

4. Fold and unfold the right side to the center crease.

**5.** Fold and unfold the left side to the last crease line made in step 4. The piece should be symmetrical—a center ridge with two creases on each side.

**6.** Lift up the top left flap. Fold the inner crease back upon itself, so it forms a ridge line.

**7.** Fold up along the outer crease line.

**8.** Repeat steps 6 and 7 on the right side, being careful to crease all the way up to the thin tips.

**9.** Collapse this shape, using a squash fold.

**10.** Lift up the left group of folds so that you can see the flat bottom flap.

**11.** Fold the outside edge in to the center, and then fold the edge back so it touches its own outer edge.

**12.** Repeat steps 10 and 11 on the right side.

**13.** Arrange the folded sides as shown in the photo.

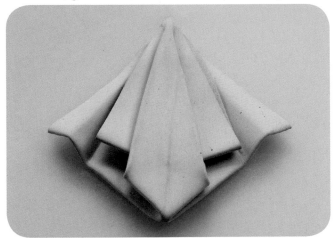

**14.** With a needle tool, make a hole for a bail. Be sure to leave enough metal clay above the hole to support the pendant.

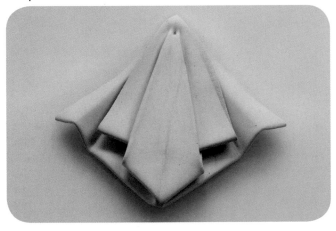

**15.** Fire the pendant flat on the kiln shelf. After firing, you can adjust the layers with chain-nose pliers, if necessary.

**16.** Add a patina, to show off the angular folds.

**17.** To attach the pendant to the cord, bend the wire in half around the largest part of the round-nose pliers, making a full circle. Slide the pendant into this loop, then twist the loop closed with the chain-nose pliers.

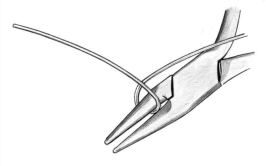

**18.** With the wires pointing straight up, begin to wrap it around the round-nose pliers, on each side of the pendant. Slide the cord through the wire wraps, then tighten them to fit loosely on the cord. Add another wrap on each side, and turn a loop on each end for a smooth finish.

# Cap Beads

Rattling around in my bead box were some matte black glass beads with an interesting grid pattern. What to do with them? Smooth, shiny, silver accent beads provide a nice contrast. Folded in a traditional origami cup pattern, these beads cup the ends of the rectangular black beads. Each easy-to-make bead uses one-fourth of a sheet.

## Materials & Supplies

**FOR THE BRACELET**

Black and clear
glass beads

Clear elastic
bead cord

**FOR THE EARRINGS**

Black and clear
glass beads

4 inches (10.2 cm)
of 20-gauge, sterling
silver wire

Sterling silver ear
posts

1. Place the one-fourth sheet in a diamond position. Fold the bottom corner to meet the opposite corner, creating a pyramid.

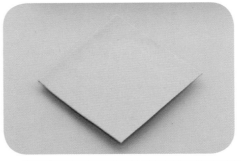

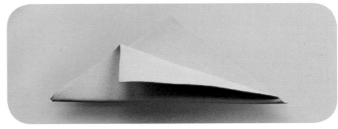

2. Fold down the top layer so that the right outside edge of the triangle rests along the bottom edge of the triangle.

3. Unfold this last fold, leaving a crease to serve as a guideline for the next fold.

4. Fold the bottom right point to the left outside edge of the triangle, lining up the point with the crease line. Press this fold firmly.

5. Turn the piece over and make the same fold, bringing the right point to the corner on the left side.

6. Fold the top single layer down over the last flap on both sides. You will have a small cup.

7. To hold the cup in place, paint a small drop of water under the point on each side and under the last two top flaps. Use very little water. Press the points to make sure they will stay in place.

8. Open up the cup and make a hole in the bottom with the needle tool.

9. Stuff a little kiln blanket inside the cup to keep it open, and fire it on the kiln shelf.

10. Tumble with stainless steel shot until the surface is bright and shiny.

11. For the bracelet shown, I threaded black, clear glass, and the silver cap beads onto clear elastic beading cord, so the bracelet would be easy to slip on and off.

12. To make the earrings, cut the wire into two 2-inch (5 cm) pieces. Thread a silver, black, and glass bead onto each wire, forming a loop in each end with the round-nose pliers. Add the ear posts.

# Freeform Piece

Once you have a grid of crease lines, you can use it to create your own unique piece—valley-folding, mountain-folding, reverse-folding, and sink-folding as the spirit moves you. This project is only one example. The fun will be in developing your own free-spirited, freeform piece.

## Materials & Supplies

Basic supply kit, page 16

Supplies for oxidizing, page 24 (optional)

1. Fold the metal clay sheet in half diagonally.

2. Fold the two layers into thirds, as shown in the photo.

3. Open the sheet, rotate it 90°, and repeat steps 1 and 2, so that the new creases are perpendicular to the first set.

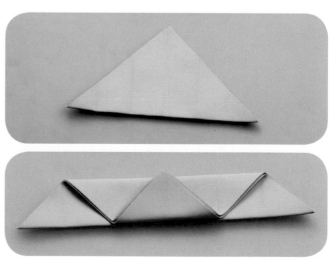

4. Open the sheet and note the grid. Fold it into thirds, using the crossing crease lines as a guide.

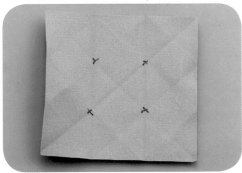

5. Turn the sheet 90°, and repeat step 4.

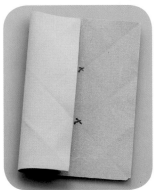 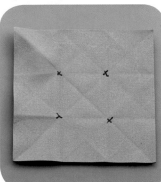

6. Valley-fold the sheet in half horizontally.

7. Open the sheet and mountain-fold the top center square.

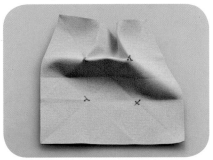

8. Now move to the square in the center of the sheet—just below the one you mountain-folded in step 7. Mountain-fold the bottom of the square. Now mountain-fold the sides, but when you do, include the triangle in each adjacent square.

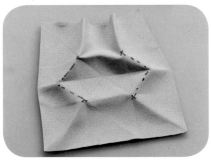

9. Sink-fold the shape you created in step 8.

**10.** Mountain-fold the diagonal lines from the lower corners of the sheet to the lower corners of the center square.

**11.** Shape these two folded corners into cones (sort of), using a modified squash fold. Don't apply too much pressure; you want the cones to remain rounded.

**12.** Sink-fold the top center square, and hold its two sides together. Make a reverse fold in both sides of the center square by pushing up, as shown, so the reverse folds form a V.

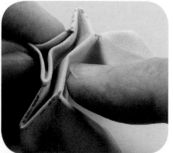

**13.** Make a reverse fold in the center of the top center square and a reverse fold between the cone shapes.

**14.** Arrange the sheet so that it has a pleasing shape, and fire it directly on the kiln shelf, supported with a kiln blanket.

**15.** Adjust the shape after firing, being careful to use any tools gently to keep from scarring the soft silver.

**16.** Add a patina, if desired. Attach either a pin finding or a bail (or both) to the back, depending on whether you want a pin or a pendant.

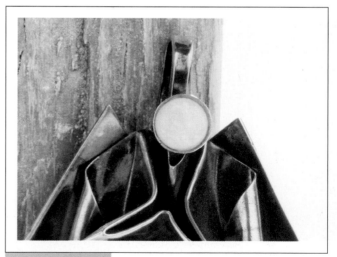

**Variation**

To lend it more strength, I soldered a sheet of silver to the back of this freeform variation. It also allowed me to add a bail topped off with a decorative stone.

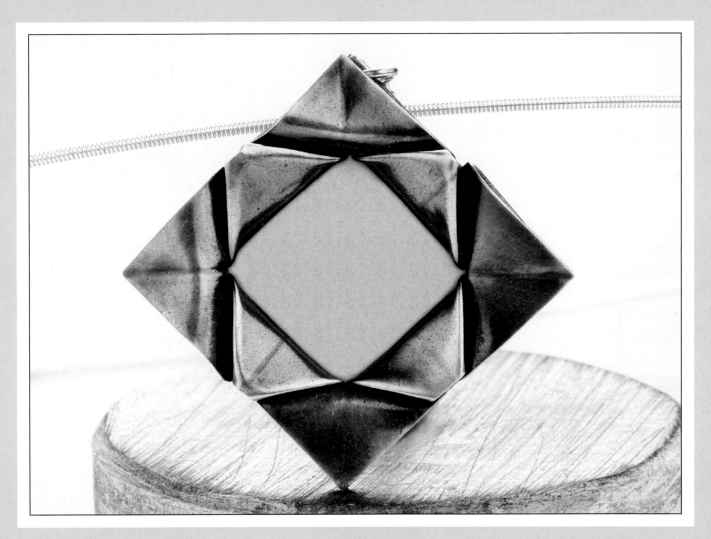

# Pinwheel
# Frame Charm

Easy to fold, this charming little frame would work
as the centerpiece of a charm bracelet.

## Materials & Supplies

Basic supply kit, page 16

Additional supplies kit, page 17

Supplies for oxidizing, page 24

2-inch (5 cm) length of 18-gauge, round, sterling silver wire

Small photo

Decoupage glue

Clear-drying epoxy (optional)

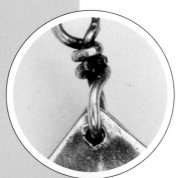

1. Make a Pinwheel (page 14).

2. Lift a corner flap so it stands along the diagonal line. Using a squash fold, open, then flatten the flap. Squash-fold the other three flaps, forming a square.

3. Working with just the top layer, lift each of the points that meet in the center, and fold it back so it rests on the opposite corner.

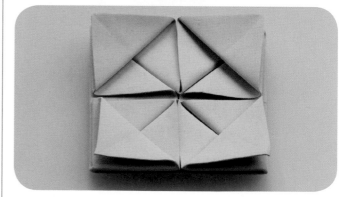

4. Now fold back the points that are left touching in the center, overlapping the previous flaps. Press the folds to define them.

5. Lift up one of the corner flaps, and make a hole for a wire bail. Let the flap fall back over the hole.

6. Fire the piece flat on the kiln shelf.

7. Using the round-nose pliers, make a bail from the 18-gauge wire, looping one end through the hole in the charm and making a loop on the other end for the chain.

8. Patina the piece.

9. To add a photo to the frame, first make a template. Cut a small square of paper, force it into frame, and trim off the excess, leaving a template that fits exactly. Set the template aside. Be sure to mark which side is up on your template.

10. Select a small photo that matches the template, or reduce a photo on your printer or copier until it's the right size.

11. Paint both sides of the picture with decoupage glue to seal it.

12. When the glue is dry, trim the photo to match the template exactly, and slide it into the frame. For a more durable finish, you can paint the photo with a two-part, clear-drying epoxy.

# Pinwheel Pod Beads

The necklace pictured has beads in three sizes, all created the same way. The large bead requires a full sheet; the medium bead uses a 2-inch (5 cm) square (just trim half an inch [1.3 cm] off two sides); and the small bead needs a quarter sheet.

## Materials & Supplies

Basic supply kit,
page 16

Additional supplies
kit, page 17

**FOR THE BEAD**

3-inch (7.6 cm)
length of 18-gauge,
round, fine silver wire
for each bead

Metal clay slip

Lump metal clay

**FOR THE NECKLACE**

2-inch (5 cm) lengths
of sterling silver
chain

1. Make a Pinwheel (page 14).

2. Lift a corner flap so it stands along the diagonal line. Using a squash fold, open, then flatten the flap. Squash-fold the other three flaps, forming a square.

3. Turn the piece over, and fold the corners to the center. All this folding will make a thick, bulky square. Press firmly to define the creases through the many layers.

**4.** Turn the piece over, making sure the folds stay in place.

**5.** Fold the top single layers back so they are flat on the work surface.

**6.** Holding the piece by its bulky center, push and fold the single layers back to meet behind the center. The flaps in the center will open, forming the pod.

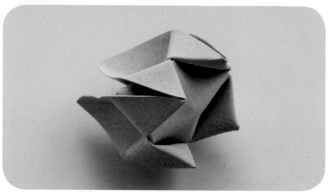

**7.** With the needle tool, make a hole in the center of the bead starting at the wide end.

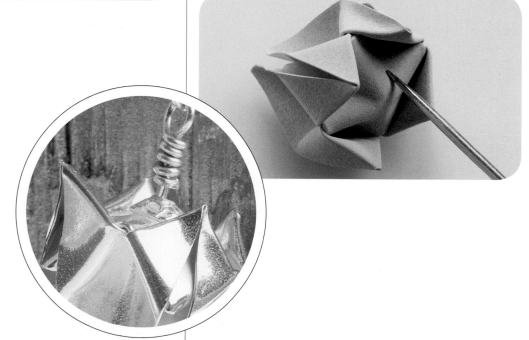

**8.** To fire, place the bead in a small container of vermiculite with the bulky end down; pour more vermiculite around the four petal shapes.

**9.** After firing, you'll need to add a wire to each end of the bead, so it can be connected to other elements later. Begin by cutting the silver wire in half, to make two pieces 1½ inches (3.8 cm) long.

**10.** Brush a little slip around the hole you made in the wide end of the bead in step 7. Press a tiny ball of lump clay over the hole. Insert a piece of the wire through the lump clay and into the hole. Allow this to dry before wiring the other end of the bead.

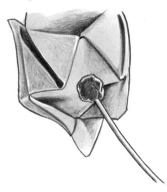

**11.** Now add the other piece of wire to the tip of the bead, where the four petals meet in the center. Wrap a little lump clay about ¼ inch (6 mm) up the wire. Brush some slip on the clay-coated tip of the wire, and insert it into the joint where the petals meet. The four petals should exert enough tension to hold the wire in place; add more slip as needed. Allow to dry.

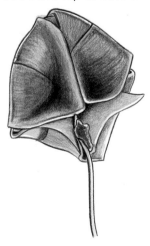

**12.** Fire the bead on the kiln shelf, with kiln blanket supporting the wires.

**13.** Finish as desired.

**14.** The beads can be used in a variety of ways. Since I wanted a necklace, I connected them to sections of sterling silver chain until I had a necklace as long as I wanted. For this easy assembly, loop the bead wire through the end of the chain and wrap the wire back around itself, using round-nose pliers.

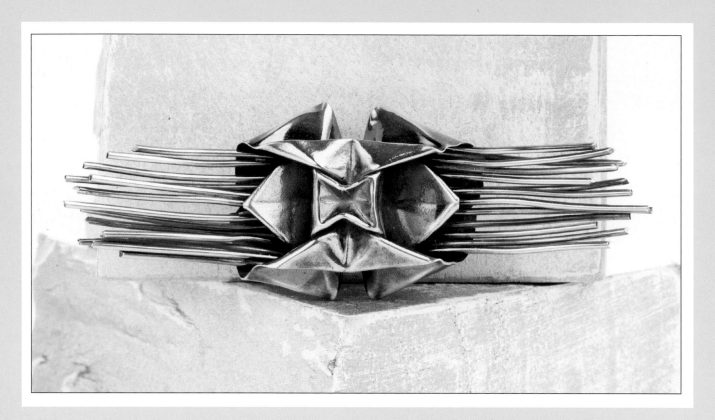

# Pinwheel Pin

This very contemporary pin could hold its own in a fine craft gallery. It's a bit challenging to fold but well worth the effort. Fiddle with a piece of paper first, and be persistent.

## Materials & Supplies

Basic supply kit,
page 16

Supplies for oxidizing,
page 24

48 inches (122 cm)
of 18-gauge, round,
sterling silver wire

Lump metal clay

Metal clay slip

Syringe metal clay

3-piece pin finding

28-gauge fine silver
bezel strip, ⅛ inch (3
mm) wide and 1½
inches (3.8 cm) long

1. Make a Pinwheel (page 14).

2. Lift a corner flap so it stands along the diagonal line. Using a squash fold, open, then flatten the flap. Squash-fold the other three flaps, forming a square.

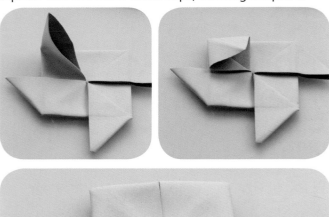

3. Turn over this compact square. Lift the two outside points on the center horizontal crease.

**4.** Bring these two points together to meet in the center. As the top layer folds up together, the bottom layer will lift with it, forming the sides.

**5.** Turn the folded piece on its side, and press firmly.

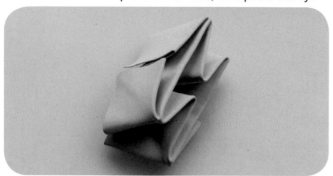

**6.** Stand this folded rectangle shape on the folds that you just completed.

**7.** Open the piece a little by pulling on the two single-layer sides (the ones that are split in the middle).

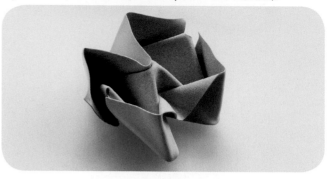

**8.** Note that, in the center of the piece, two single-sheet flaps come to a point in the middle of the center fold, almost meeting. Fold back each of these points, which will become straight edges, making a reverse fold.

**9.** Holding the piece by the bottom, fold over and unfold the center point in both directions, about 1/8 to 1/4 inch (3 to 6 mm) from the tip. Push and spread the folded tip into a small square, and make a sink fold in the center, following the creases that you made by folding and unfolding the tip.

10. For added detail, make a reverse fold in the middle of the two sides that are on the same side of the square as the reverse folds in step 8. Press the entire model shut to make a positive crease line for the sink fold.

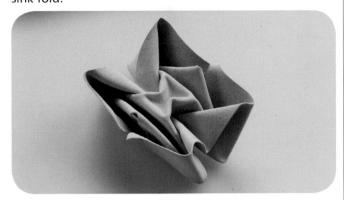

11. Place the folded shape on the kiln shelf. The two split sides will be the back of the pin. Arrange the piece so the folded ends of the two split sides don't quite touch each other in the middle of the piece (turn it over to see). I like to leave a space here to keep the overall piece in a rectangular shape.

12. Tuck some fiber blanket under the edges and the inner protruding triangles so the piece retains its shape during firing, and fire on the kiln shelf.

13. Cut the wire into 24 pieces, each about 2 inches (5 cm) long.

14. Make a narrow roll of metal clay, about the diameter of heavy string. On one side of the folded piece, force the roll into the gap between the protruding inner triangle and the back of the piece. Paint a generous amount of slip in this space, on top of the metal clay. Poke 12 of the wires into the clay so they are wedged in and held firm. Allow to dry, then repeat on the other side.

15. To support the pin findings, I attached a 1-inch (2.5 cm) strip of rectangular fine-silver bezel wire to the back with syringe metal clay. The findings were then attached to the bezel wire, also with syringe clay.

16. Fire the assembled pin in a can of vermiculite, or use a kiln blanket to support the findings and decorative wires.

17. Trim the wires to random lengths, then brush, oxidize, and tumble the entire piece.

# My Star Pendant

This compact, very three-dimensional piece has a smooth, relatively flat back that makes it ideal for a pendant. Because the silver folds rise high above the base, they reflect the light with special brilliance.

## Materials & Supplies

Basic supply kit,
page 16

Jump ring

1. Fold a Preliminary Base (page 11), and position it with the open end facing toward you.

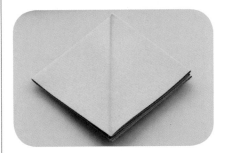

2. Lift a flap upright, so it stands on the diagonal, then open the flap and make a squash fold.

3. Squash-fold the other three flaps.

 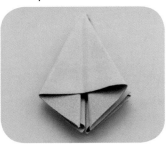

4. Fold over a long, vertical flap so a smooth surface faces you.

5. Fold up the top single layer as shown in the photo, making a small triangular flap. Repeat on the three remaining sides. Note: This is the basic pyramid of the piece; take a good look at it, on all sides. You will be remaking it later, in modified form.

6. Fold the entire piece in half by folding the tip to the center of the pyramid's base.

7. To make sure that this halfway crease is well defined through all layers, make the same crease three more times, by opening at each triangle flap and folding the pyramid in half.

8. Open up the entire sheet into an octagon, leaving the four small triangular flaps folded over.

9. Mountain-fold the crease lines that form a smaller, central octagon.

10. Mountain-fold the line that goes from each corner of the large octagon to the central, smaller octagon. (These creases are already mountain creases, but redefining them will help with the next step.)

**11.** Sink-fold the central octagon and remake the basic pyramid, with the tip and central octagon folded inside. You'll be following the valley and mountain creases already established at the outer edges. (Don't worry about the folds in the sunken area; they'll be flattened later.)

**12.** Fold over a vertical flap so that a smooth surface faces you.

**13.** Now fold up a lower corner so that the bottom edge almost comes to the center; repeat with the other corner.

**14.** Repeat step 13 for the three remaining smooth sides.

**15.** Place the piece with its large end down, and push down on the center, spreading the piece out on the work surface, keeping the three-dimensional folds in place.

**16.** As if by magic, the star will open, radiating from a central point, while the back remains relatively flat.

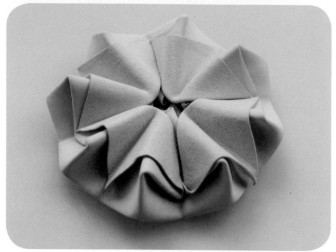

**17.** Make a hole for a bail in the center of one flat edge with the needle tool.

**18.** Fire the piece flat on the kiln shelf, and polish it to a brilliant silver.

**19.** Insert the jump ring through the hole in the pendant, and attach it to the narrow chain of your choice.

This big, dramatic ring, with its multiple silver folds, is great fun to wear. My version is topped with a cubic zirconia, but any kiln-safe stone will do. Prepare for multiple compliments!

## Materials & Supplies

Basic supply kit, page 16

Additional supplies kit, page 17

5 mm, kiln-safe stone

High-density, low-fire metal clay

.999 silver ring band

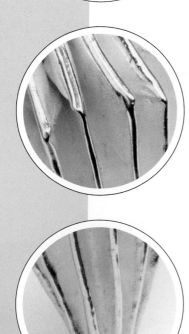

1. Fold the first four steps of the Frog Base (see page 12).

2. Fold over the large vertical flap, and repeat Frog steps 2 through 4 on the three remaining flaps. This will create eight flaps.

3. Fold over one of the flaps so that a smooth diamond shape is facing up.

**4.** Turn the piece over to sit on this flat side, and arrange the flaps so they stand up, spaced more or less equally from each other.

**5.** Tuck small bits of kiln blanket between the flaps to maintain their spacing, and fire the piece on the kiln shelf.

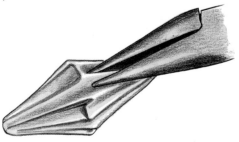

**6.** After firing, true up the spacing with chain-nose pliers.

**7.** Make a ball bezel for the stone with the lump metal clay. (See Making a Setting for a Stone, page 19.)

**8.** Attach the bezelled stone to the end of the origami form with slip, and allow it to dry.

**9.** To attach the origami form to the ring band, first make a small patty of lump metal clay and press the band into it. This creates an indentation the proper size and shape for the band to fit into. Trim off the extra clay, and attach the patty to the back of the origami with thick slip.

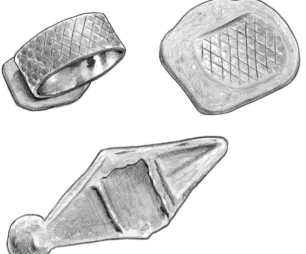

**10.** Paint slip on the concave patty, and press in the band. Trim any clay that extends beyond the origami form. Be sure to check that the long origami piece sits perpendicular to the band.

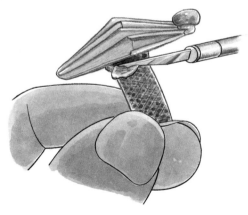

**11.** Allow the assembled ring to dry, then refine any rough areas with a salon file. After filing or sanding, remove any clay dust from the surface of the stone with a damp cotton swab.

**12.** Support the top of the ring with a kiln blanket, and fire it on the kiln shelf. (See Firing with Stones, page 22.)

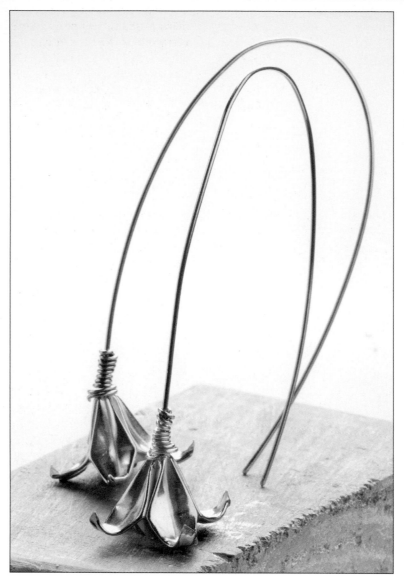

# Lily
# Earrings

The Lily Pin (page 84) uses a full-size sheet of metal clay. These little earrings each use one-fourth of a sheet. Working with a quarter sheet is very similar to working with a full-size one—just smaller. The delicate earrings can tolerate fewer folds before they become too thick to work with, so they have fewer and simpler moves than the pin.

## Materials & Supplies

Basic supply kit,
page 16

Additional supplies
kit, page 17

10 inches (25.4 cm)
of 20-gauge, round,
sterling silver wire

4 inches (10.2 cm)
of 24-gauge, round,
sterling silver wire

1. Begin by folding the quarter sheet of metal clay into a Frog Base (see page 12). Position the base with the open end away from you.

2. Fold over all four vertical flaps so that only smooth, unbroken surfaces are visible.

3. Fold each petal back.

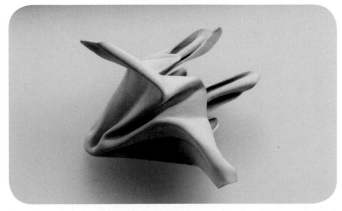

4. You may need to give an additional pinch to the inside points of the smaller triangles, which need to stay folded in half. The flower petals will radiate around a square cone.

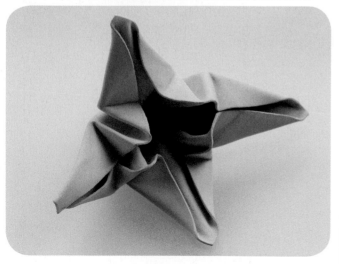

5. Make a hole for the stem in the base of the lily, using a needle tool.

6. Fire the lily facedown on the removable kiln shelf.

7. Make small adjustments with your fingers after the piece is fired, if necessary—easy to do with the delicate sheet.

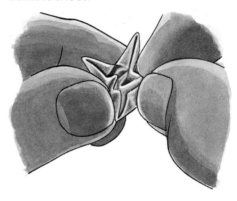

8. Finish as desired. I like a bright silver finish for this earring, so I tumbled it for 20 minutes before assembling the earring. If you prefer, you can add a patina.

9. To make the ear wire that is a continuous part of the design, first cut both pieces of the wire in half. Make a small loop in one end of the 20-gauge wire with the round-nose pliers; this will be the stem. Hook the 24-gauge wire through this loop, and wrap it around the stem several times, close to the loop.

10. File the hole in the lily to an oval shape, and run both wires through the hole so the loop is tucked inside the lily. Wind the smaller wire around the stem and up onto the flower. Trim off the excess, and tuck the end into the wrapping.

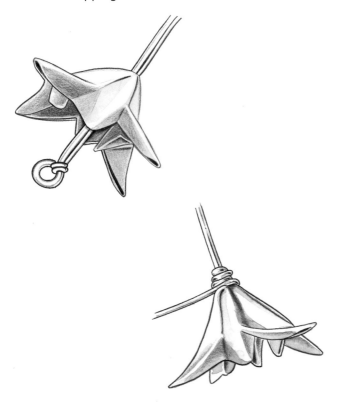

11. Decide how far you want the earring dangle from the ear, then bend the wire into an open oval the appropriate length. Trim off any excess. File the end of the wire that will go through the ear so there are no rough edges.

# Lily Pin

The beautiful origami lily is one of my favorite traditional folds
because it is so enchanting in silver. This four-petal flower grows
into three dimensions from the flat square sheet with some
simple folds and a few complex ones.

## Materials & Supplies

Basic supply kit,
page 16

Additional supplies kit,
page 17

6 inches (15.2 cm) of
14-gauge, round, sterling
silver wire

6 inches (15.2 cm) of
22-gauge, round, sterling
silver wire

6 inches (15.2 cm)
of 18-gauge, half-hard,
round, sterling silver wire

Ball-peen hammer

1. Begin by folding the Frog Base (page 12).

2. Turn the base so that the open end points away from you, and fold over one vertical flap to cover the little triangular fold. A smooth, diamond-shaped surface will face you.

3. Fold over the right and left sides from the bottom point to meet in the middle. Press this fold firmly because the metal clay sheet is very thick, and you want it to remember this fold and stay put.

4. Repeat step 3 for the remaining three sides.

5. To make the lily bloom, pick it up by the base and open out the petals. Those little triangles of metal clay may need another pinch to get them to sit between the four petals.

6. Using a needle tool, make a small hole for the stem in the bottom of the lily.

7. Fire the lily facedown in a container of vermiculite. Position the petals so they curve back slightly; the cone of the lily doesn't need support.

8. After firing, use your fingers and the round-nose pliers to adjust the position of the petals, if necessary. For the pin, it's best to roll the tips of the petals under, so they won't snag on fabric when worn.

9. Wire brush the lily to make it shine. The final polishing will be done after the pin is complete.

10. With a round file, make the hole in the base of the lily large enough to hold the 14-gauge and 22-gauge wires. Using the round-nose pliers, form a ¼-inch (6 mm) loop on one end of the 14-gauge wire. Make a small crook in one end of the thin, 22-gauge wire, hook it into the 14-gauge loop, and wrap around it at least twice. Feed both wires through the hole in the base of the lily, so the loop is deep inside the throat of the flower.

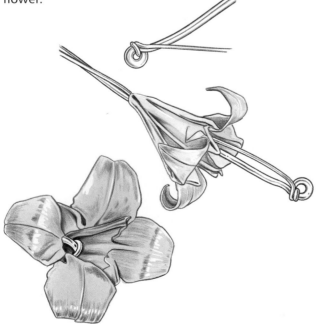

11. At the base of the lily, bend the 22-gauge wire at a right angle and wrap it around the heavier wire stem, starting ⅛ inch (3 mm) below the lily and continuing ¼ inch (6 mm) up the flower. Trim off any excess, and tuck the end inside the wrapping.

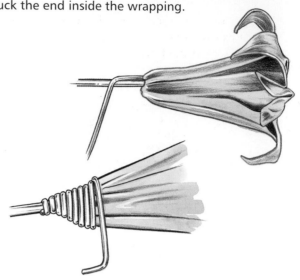

12. Use the round-nosed pliers to make an open spiral on the end of the stem, and texture the stem with a ball-peen hammer.

13. Make a one-piece pin with clasp, using the half-hard, 18-gauge wire, incorporating the clasp into the stem of the lily. To begin, wrap two full circles around the round-nosed pliers. To make the catch, open out the second loop, leaving a full circle on the tip. The pin will catch against this circle.

**14.** One-half inch (1.3 cm) below the catch, bend the wire into a right angle and wrap it snugly around the stem, beginning at the base of the flower and continuing down the stem for an inch (2.5 cm).

**15.** To form the spring joint, bend the wire at a right angle to the base and make a complete circle the same height as the catch at the flower end of the clasp. Trim off the pin and file it to a point.

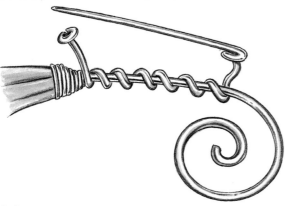

**16.** Polish and finish as desired.

**TIP:** Don't have the half-hard sterling wire for the pin? Work-harden 18-gauge, round, sterling silver wire for a stiffer pin by tapping it with a hammer against a metal block.

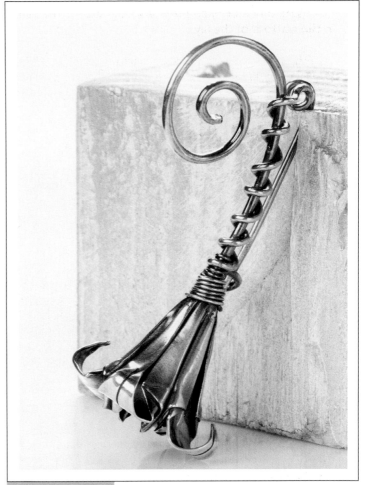

The oxidized finish on this piece adds depth and dimension to the folds.

# Twisted Beads

With its eye-catching shape, this elongated little bead can serve as a spacer for other, more elaborate beads or hold its own as a full partner. Each bead is made from one-fourth sheet of metal clay for the twist, with tiny balls of lump clay at top and bottom.

## Materials & Supplies

Basic supply kit, page 16

Additional supplies kit, page 17

Supplies for oxidizing, page 24

**FOR THE BEAD**

2-inch (5 cm) length of very straight, 20-gauge brass or copper wire, or a pin stem from a 3-piece pin finding

Low-fire lump metal clay

Large plastic straw

Metal clay slip

**FOR THE BRACELET**

Open-link chain bracelet

2-inch (5 cm) 18-gauge head pin for each bead

Additional beads as desired

1. Begin by folding a Preliminary Base (see page 11).

2. Place the base with the open end facing you, and fold the right side of each flap to the center.

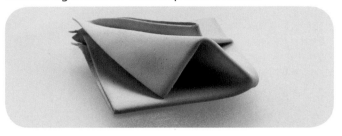

3. Pick up the folded piece by the tips at the open end, holding them together. Grasp the closed end in your other hand and, making sure the flaps go around in the same direction, twist in the direction of the flaps with one hand and the opposite way with the other.

4. Set the piece on the work surface and allow it to relax a little.

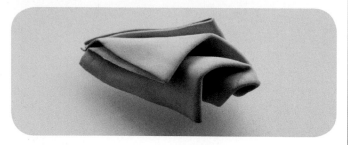

5. Push down on the tip of the folded end, to provide a bit of a flat surface.

6. Make a hole in this flat spot with a needle tool.

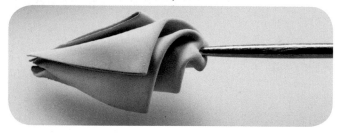

7. Fire the bead on the kiln shelf.

8. Coat the pin stem or brass wire with olive oil, and run it through the center of the fired bead, to open the hole and support the construction of the bead.

9. Roll out a small lump of metal clay three playing cards thick, and use the large straw to cut disks of clay.

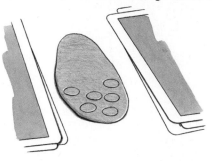

10. Grease your fingers and palms with olive oil, and roll these disks into little balls. Make two balls for each bead.

11. Thread a ball onto the oiled pin, add the twist, and add another ball. Brush a little slip on the joints between the balls and the twist.

12. Leave the bead on the pin to fire, to keep the holes open and lined up with each other. The metal clay won't stick to the pin or the wire, because the pure silver is a different metal. Be sure to allow the lump clay to dry before firing.

13. Remove the pin after firing, then polish and patina the bead as desired.

14. To assemble the bracelet, thread a head pin through the bead, loop the pin through a link in the bracelet, and wrap it around itself. Add the remaining beads (or stack of beads) in the same way.

**TIP:** Since I planned to combine Twisted Beads with hematite beads, I wanted a shiny, antique gray finish that would complement the hematite. To achieve that, I left the beads in a liver of sulfur solution until they were uniformly black, then rubbed the patina off the higher areas with fine pumice powder. After tumbling, the beads' brilliant luster matched the hematite almost exactly.

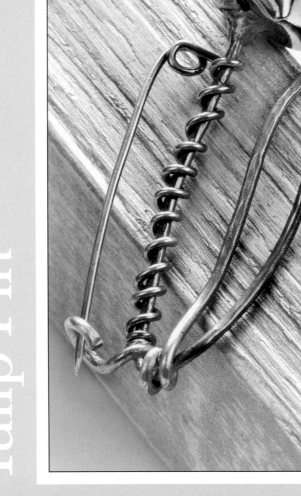

# Tulip Pin

This origami tulip makes a sturdy, compact flower that works well with a wire-wrapped stem and a long, graceful leaf. There's even a ready-made hole in the tulip's base for attaching the stem.

## Materials & Supplies

Basic supply kit, page 16

Additional supplies kit, page 17

Supplies for oxidizing, page 24

7 inches (17.8 cm) of 16-gauge, round, sterling silver wire

6 inches (15.2 cm) of 18-gauge, round, sterling silver wire

Metal clay slip

Lump metal clay

Ball-peen hammer

Tulip Pin

1. Begin by folding a Waterbomb Base (see page 13). Position the base with the open bottom of the pyramid toward you.

2. Pick up one corner of the top layer, and fold the flap up so the open edge falls on the center crease. Repeat with the other flap. Make sure both sides meet at the top of the pyramid, and press flat.

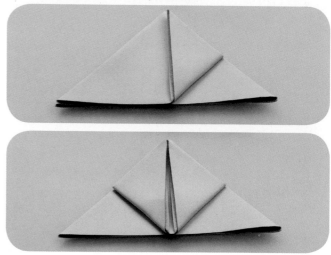

3. Turn the piece over and repeat step 2, forming a square in the diamond position.

**4.** Swing over a top flap so that the square has only a crease line in the center.

**5.** Turn the piece over and repeat step 4.

**NOTE:** When turning the folded piece over, make sure that you turn from left to right, not from top to bottom. This will keep the small opening toward you and the closed top pointing away.

**6.** Fold over the left flap from the top point so it forms a triangle that reaches a little past the centerline.

**7.** Fold the right flap over and place it into the small pocket formed by the left flap.

**8.** Turn the piece over and repeat steps 6 and 7.

# Pocket Pendant

Most origami starts with a square, but much can be done with rectangles, as well. These three pieces all begin with a half sheet of metal clay—in other words, a rectangle. Their fluid lines result from the material's elasticity; it will stretch and curve, as well as fold. The Pocket Pendant's three-dimensional pocket offers a perfect setting for a bright glass cabochon.

## Materials & Supplies

Lump metal clay

Metal clay slip

10 mm dichroic glass
cabochon

Epoxy

1. Start with one-half of a metal clay sheet. Valley-fold this rectangle in half, long sides together. Open it out flat, leaving a well-defined crease down the center.

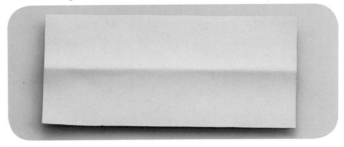

2. Mountain-fold the sheet in half, short sides together, making a shorter rectangle. Crease firmly.

3. Fold two small triangular flaps by bringing each half of the folded edge to the center crease line. Open the triangles, and use the crease lines to make an inside reverse fold on each side.

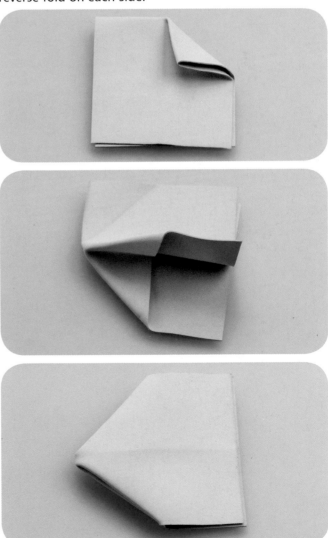

**4.** Working with only the top layer, valley-fold one corner of the rectangular end into a triangular flap, so that the bottom edge rests on the center crease line. Repeat with the other corner, to form a point.

**5.** Valley-fold both sides of this point so the folded edges fall along the center crease line.

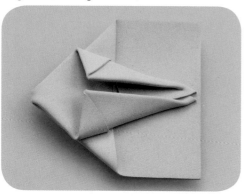

**6.** Repeat these folds once more, making the point very narrow. Because the long point has lots of layers, be sure to press it firmly so it stays folded.

**7.** Slowly lift up on the thin point, folding it all the way back so that it points in the opposite direction.

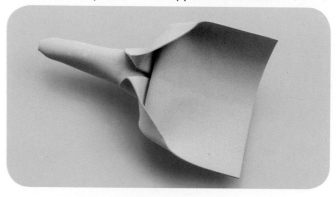

**8.** Fold up the lower single layer so the bottom edge meets in the center, making a pointed tip. Press this thick fold to make it stay put. (If it does relax and begins to unfold, just refold it tight to get your thin point back.)

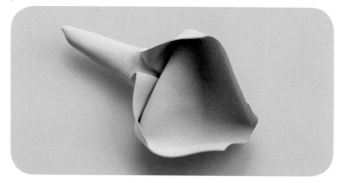

**9.** Turn the piece over and valley-fold the tip from step 8, then fold it back, creating the effect shown.

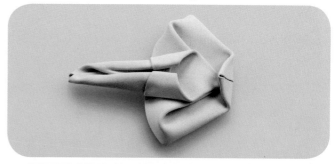

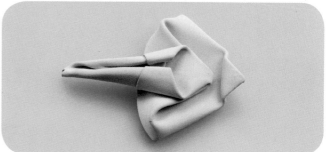

**10.** To make a pocket for the cabochon, turn the piece back over and fold up the edges of the single-layer flaps, as shown.

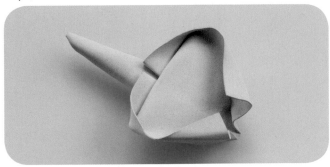

**11.** Holding the folded piece by both points, pull gently to develop the pocket in the center, with a curved edge on each side.

**12.** Fire on the removable kiln shelf, with pieces of kiln blanket supporting each side of the pocket ledge.

**13.** To make a bail, roll out a small log of lump metal clay, and attach both ends to the back of the fired piece with a generous amount of slip. Add a small ball of clay, to give it a finished look.

**14.** Roll out two more balls of clay, and attach them to the front of the piece with slip, as shown.

**15.** Fire a second time.

**16.** Patina the piece.

**17.** Epoxy the glass cabochon into the pocket.

# Flip-Side
# Pocket Pendant

Halfway through folding the Pocket Pendant (page 96), I discovered that happily, with some alternate moves, the back was just as appealing as the front—hence the flip-side reference.

## Materials & Supplies

Basic supply kit,
page 16

Additional supplies
kit, page 17

Supplies for oxidizing,
page 24

Lump metal clay

Metal clay slip

Fine silver bail

6 mm fine silver bezel
cup

Four pieces of fine
silver shot

6 mm decorative
stone

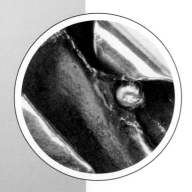

1. Follow steps 1 through 6 for the Pocket Pendant (page 97).

2. Valley-fold both corners of the single layer to the center crease line, which is under the folded narrow piece that was created in earlier steps. The bottom edges of the single layer will meet in the center.

3. Slowly lift up on the long, thin point, folding it all the way back so that it points in the opposite direction. Do not press or crease this move, but allow the metal clay to create a curved line.

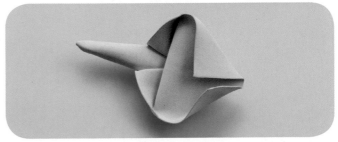

**7.** After firing, use the round-nose pliers to curl in the corners of the sheet.

**8.** If the thick end of the long point opened during firing, close it with your fingers or with chain-nose pliers.

**4.** Turn the piece over; this is now the front.

**5.** Place the folded piece on the work surface, and allow the single layer that you folded in step 2 to unfold forward, leaving two diagonal ridges.

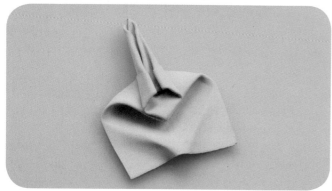

**6.** Fire the piece flat on the kiln shelf.

**9.** With bits of lump clay and a little slip, attach the jump ring to the back of the pendant for a bail and the bezel cup to the front.

**10.** For a bit of extra decoration, add the silver shot, positioned as shown.

**11.** After the slip and clay have dried, fire the piece a second time.

**12.** Patina the pendant.

**13.** After all finishing is complete, insert the stone into the bezel cup, and secure it by tightening the edges of the cup with a burnishing tool.

# Arrowhead Earrings

I know it may not look like it, but this pendant is close kin with the Pocket Pendant (page 96) since to create either one you follow the same first seven steps. While experimenting with designs, I found that with one good tug, the folded shape of the in-process Pocket Pendant would stretch into a hollow form, thus becoming the Arrowhead Earrings.

## Materials & Supplies

Basic supply kit, page 16

Additional supplies kit, page 17

4 inches (10.2 cm) of 24-gauge, round, sterling silver wire

Sterling silver ear wires

1. Follow steps 1 through 7 for the Pocket Pendant (page 96).

2. Fold the corners of the single layer to the back with mountain folds, forming a point.

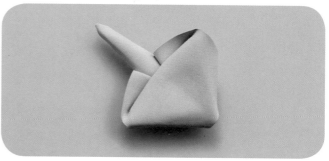

3. Pick up the piece by both ends. Tug in opposite directions until the stress on the folded shape forces the centerline to lift, and a small, concave space begins to form.

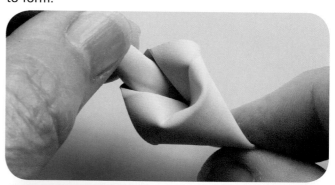

4. Pinch the edges of this concave space to define an angular, arrowhead shape.

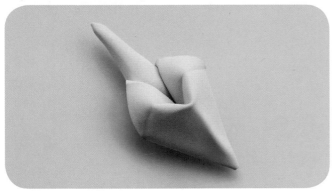

5. Lay the piece on your work surface, and straighten and align the sides.

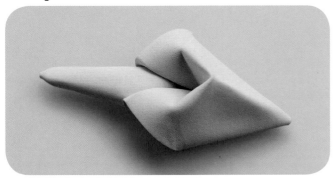

6. Make a hole through the thick point with a pin.

7. Fire the piece on its back. It needs no support.

8. Finish as desired.

9. To assemble the earring, insert a 2-inch (5 cm) length of wire through the hole made in step 6, and wrap the wire up the earring to its tip. With the round-nose pliers, form a loop in the end to hold the ear wire.

# Reverse Fold Earrings

These light, bright dangles are made with a series of
reverse folds—a fold that is fun to do, and easier to do
than to explain. Try the earring in paper first, before
embarking on silver. Fold both earrings at the same time,
so they'll be as identical as possible.

## Materials & Supplies

Basic supply kit,
page 16

Additional supplies
kit, page 17

4 inches (10.2 cm)
of 20-gauge, round,
sterling silver wire

**TIP:** For this project, a stiffer paper—for example, origami paper or computer printer paper—works better, because it retains the creases well.

1. Each earring uses half of a metal clay sheet. Begin by cutting the sheet into two rectangular strips, and follow the same steps for each earring.

2. Mountain-fold the strip in half, long sides together. Press the crease firmly with your finger.

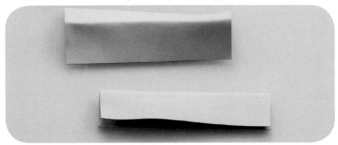

3. Fold and unfold the strip in half, short ends together.

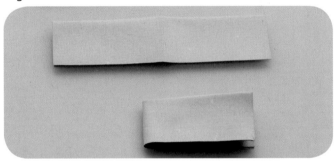

4. Sight a line between the center point of the folded edge and the lower right corner, and valley-fold along that line, forming a triangle. To make this diagonal crease show up in the thick clay sheet, fold the triangle to the back of the strip as well, and press again.

5. Fold up the part of the triangle that projects below the lower edge of the strip, so that the fold line is level with the bottom of the strip. Turn the piece over, and make the same fold on the other side, to define the crease clearly.

6. To make the first (and largest) reverse fold, hold the piece at its midpoint, and open out the folded end. Press down on the center crease, to turn it into a valley fold. The diagonal folds will obligingly become mountain folds.

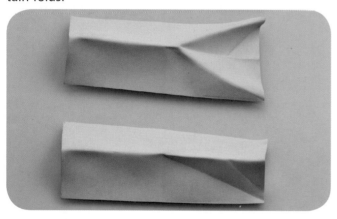

7. Make the second reverse fold—this time on the smaller triangle—by doing the opposite: mountain-fold the short center crease, encouraging the short diagonals to become valley folds.

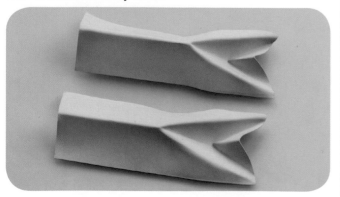

8. To make the third reverse fold—this one on the tiny flap that sticks out when the folded piece is closed—fold the tiny flap over, even with the slanted edge of the piece, then open it and reverse it.

**9.** Put the folded piece down on the work surface half-folded, and press firmly. To make those long diagonal creases shown in the photo, fold over the pointed half of the piece along the centerline of the first, largest reverse fold. You'll feel all the inside flaps folding with you.

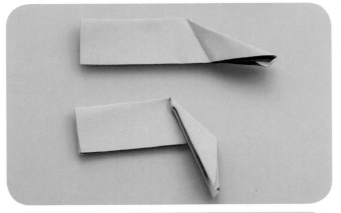

**10.** Fold the other half of the piece into fourths by folding it in half, then in half again. Mentally number the resulting creases 1 through 4, with 1 being the center crease. (You might actually number them on your paper model.)

**11.** Working between creases 1 and 2, valley-fold the top edge of the piece so it falls along crease 2. This will create a diagonal line parallel to the one you made in step 9.

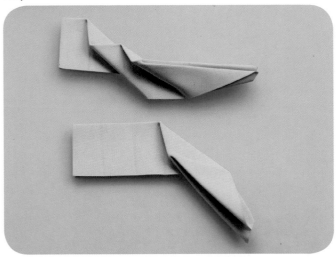

**12.** Turn the piece over and make the same fold again: working between creases 2 and 3, fold the long edge of the piece so it falls along crease 3, to make a third diagonal line.

**13.** Continue this same process to the end of the piece. The last folded edge will fall along the outer edge of the piece.

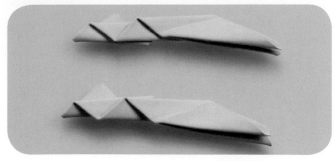

**14.** Open out the folded sheet, but don't press it flat.

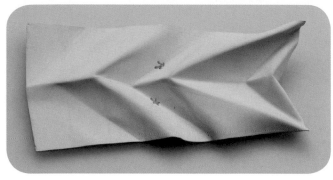

**15.** Pinch up the crease lines of the large reverse fold and the diagonal lines on each side of it (the lines you made in step 9). Both these lines should be mountain folds.

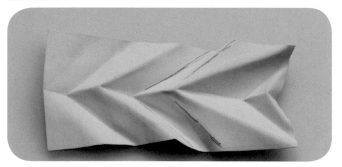

**16.** Now proceed with reverse folds along the remaining diagonal lines to the end of the piece, alternating valley and mountain folds. (Hint: Crease 1 will mark a mountain fold, crease 2 a valley fold, and crease 3 a mountain fold.) The last fold will leave two triangular flaps on the corners; turn these under.

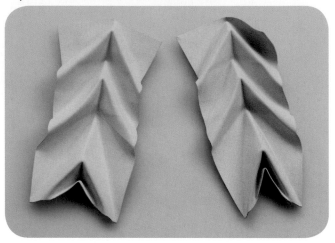

**17.** Turn the piece over and further define the folds with a little pinch. Don't worry if the piece loses its shape for a moment, because the metal clay sheet will remember how it was folded. Hold both ends, and reshape the piece.

18. Make a hole with the needle tool for the ear wire.

19. Fire the earrings on the kiln shelf with pieces of kiln blanket under the large open folds.

20. Use your fingers or chain-nose pliers to do any final shaping that's needed.

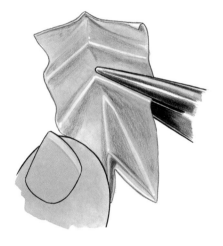

21. To make the findings, cut two 2-inch (5 cm) pieces of silver wire. With round-nose pliers, make a loop on the tip of each wire, then form a bend about ¼ inch (6 mm) from the loop. Because the hole for the wire is tucked under the earring's folded edge, this bend will help it hang nicely.

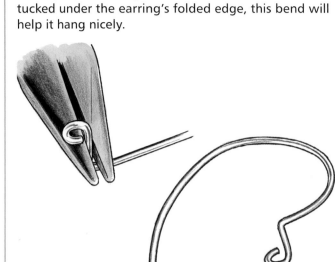

22. Bend the ear wires around a rounded tool handle to shape their curves, and smooth the clipped ends with a file or micro paper. Insert the wires from the front.

23. Brush the finished earrings with soapy water and a brass wire brush to burnish a shine. For an even brighter shine, tumble them with stainless steel shot.

# Samurai Pin

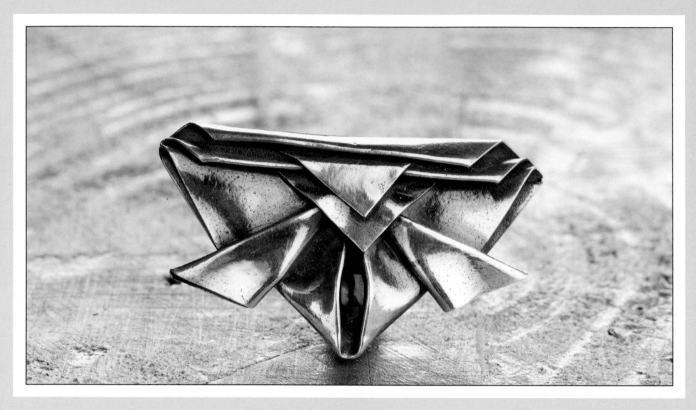

A traditional origami pattern, the Samurai Helmet uses simple folds to create a series of triangular layers in an interesting combination. I've adapted the last few folds to create an easy-to-make silver pin, set off by a kiln-safe synthetic stone.

## Materials & Supplies

Basic supply kit,
page 16

Supplies for oxidizing,
page 24

6 mm round, blue,
synthetic sapphire (or
stone of your choice)

One-piece pin finding

Epoxy

1. Place the metal clay sheet on the work surface in a diamond position.

2. Fold up the corner pointing toward you to meet the opposite corner, forming a pyramid. Make sure the corners and edges match, then press the fold firmly.

3. Fold the two sides up so they meet in the center and reach the top of the pyramid. Press firmly.

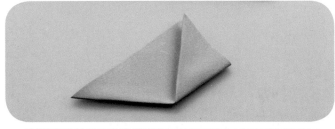

4. Fold down the two top flaps at their halfway lines, so that their tips meet at the bottom.

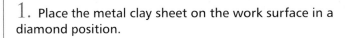
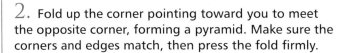

113

5. Fold each flap up so that the top edge extends beyond the piece and is more or less parallel to the half-way line. You can see the helmet beginning to form.

6. Now fold the top layer of the pyramid triangle down, leaving a small excess edge—about ¼ inch (6 mm).

7. Carefully fold the extra ¼-inch (6 mm) edge down to create a lip.

8. Fold the remaining pyramid flap forward in the same way. You may want to pick it up so you can pinch this fold.

9. Fold this extra edge down in the same way.

10. You may tuck a stone in the folds. Remember that the clay will shrink during firing, exposing more of the stone.

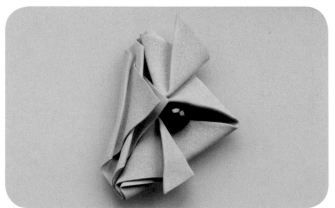

11. Fire the piece on the kiln shelf with strips of kiln blanket over the flaps that extend out, to keep the metal clay sheet from relaxing and losing its shape during firing.

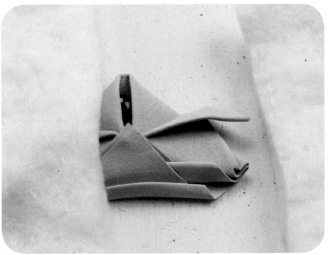

12. Patina the piece, to highlight the three-dimensional folds.

13. Attach the one-piece pin finding with epoxy or attach fine silver findings before firing.

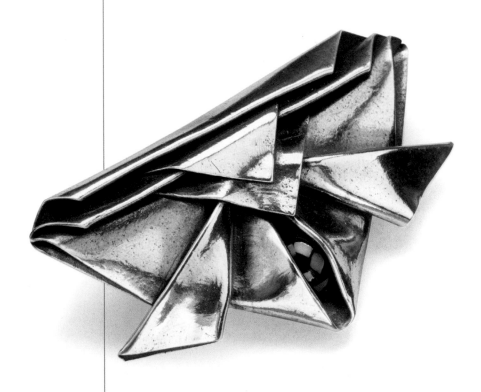

# Winged Earrings

Metal clay sheet is feather-light after it is fired, which makes it perfect for large, flirty earrings that flash silver as you move. With a few simple folds, you can make these origami-inspired, winged earrings.

## Materials & Supplies

Basic supply kit,
page 16

Additional supplies
kit, page 17

4 inches (10.2 cm)
of 20-gauge, round,
sterling silver wire

Ear posts

1. Cut the metal clay sheet in half. Each strip will make one earring and will follow the same instructions.

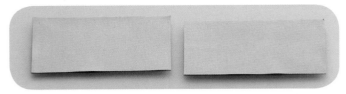

2. Valley-fold the strip in half, long sides together. I'll refer to this as the long fold for the rest of the instructions.

3. Fold and unfold the strip in half, short ends together.

4. Imagine lines between the center of the long fold and the bottom corners of the clay sheet, and valley-fold along those lines. Unfold these flaps, leaving crease lines for the next step.

**5.** Now pick up the sheet at the center of the long fold and open out one end to its original width. The creases will form a triangle, with a ridge crease in the center and the valley creases forming each side. By pushing down on the center, reverse-fold this triangle, so that the center ridge crease becomes a valley and the outer creases become ridges. The reversed triangle will protrude below the rest of the clay. Repeat this reverse fold on the other end.

**6.** Bring the two ends together so the inside flaps meet in the center. You will have created an extra flap on both sides of the top center. Fold this flap to one side.

**7.** Spread the little flap open with the needle tool, and squash-fold it. Repeat on the reverse side. Because of metal clay's elasticity, the squash-folded flap will bounce up a bit, adding extra dimension.

8. Make a hole in the top of the piece with the needle tool.

9. Place the earrings on the removable kiln shelf, using short strips of kiln blanket to help the wings stay open, and fire them.

10. Make any needed adjustments to the fired pieces with chain-nose pliers. Because metal clay shrinks during firing, you may need to true up the holes with the needle tool.

11. For each earring, cut a 2-inch (5 cm) length of sterling wire, and make a loop on one end with the round-nose pliers. To make the earring hang straight, adjust the loop so it is centered over the wire. Thread the wire in from the bottom, and tug the loop up so it is hidden in the folds.

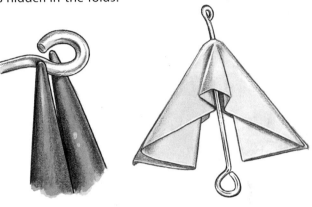

12. Make a similar loop on the other end of the wire, and center it.

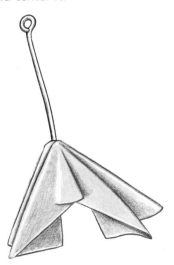

13. Patina the earrings to show off the folded lines, and attach the ear posts.

## Twin Pin

This stunning pin is composed of two sheets of metal clay folded into identical shapes, then joined in the center and topped with a square-cut stone. The folds follow the first few steps of the traditional Cicada pattern, but not far enough into the sequence for the insect to take shape.

## Materials & Supplies

Basic supply kit,
page 16

Additional supplies
kit, page 17

Lump metal clay

6 mm square cubic
zirconia (or stone of
your choice)

Metal clay slip

Syringe clay
(optional)

Plastic roller and
playing cards

3-piece pin finding

1. Place a metal clay sheet on the work surface in a diamond position.

2. Fold up the corner pointing toward you to meet the opposite corner, forming a pyramid. Press the fold firmly.

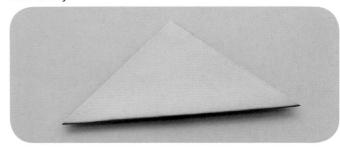

3. Fold the right and left sides up so that they meet in the center and at the top.

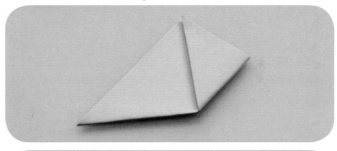

4. Fold down the two top flaps so their tips extend beyond the lower edge of the model, forming a V-shaped opening on each side of the center fold line.

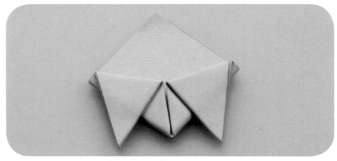

**5.** Fold the top layer of the original triangle down.

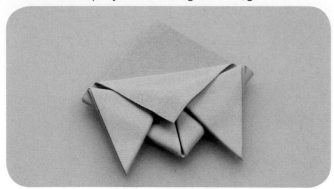

**6.** Fold the remaining layer of the triangle down, stopping short of the previous triangle. Press these folds firmly.

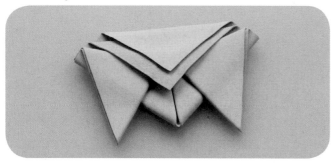

**7.** Repeat steps 1 through 6 for the second metal clay sheet.

**8.** Fire the two folded pieces flat on the kiln shelf.

**9.** To prepare the stone, put a little olive oil or balm on your hands, place an olive-size lump of metal clay on a nonstick sheet, and roll it out seven playing cards thick. Press the stone into the clay, deep enough for the clay to rise slightly above it. Trim around the stone, leaving a bezel ⅛ inch (3 mm) wide, and set it aside to dry. The best time to refine the bezel is before it's fired in place, so once it's dry, sand it with a salon file.

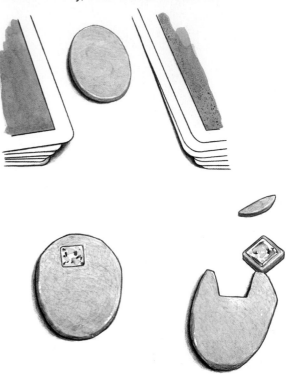

**10.** Now it's time to put everything together. Roll a log of metal clay about ¼ inch (6 mm) in diameter and long enough to span the pieces' thick, folded edges. Cut a wedge point on each end of the roll.

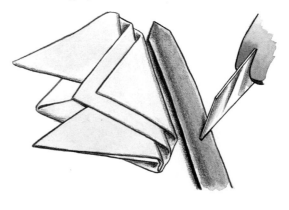

11. Paint the folded edges with metal clay slip, and press them into the log. Brush distilled water on these joints, to help the slip flow into the porous fired sheet. Add more wet slip along the joints to strengthen them, but not so much that the shape is lost.

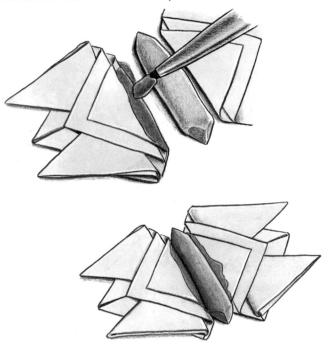

12. Paint slip on the back of the bezelled stone and on the place it will sit. Press the stone and bezel into position. Make sure that the bezel has slip on it wherever it touches the fired clay, and that it is well seated in the unfired log.

13. When all joints are dry, turn the piece over and patch any openings with slip.

14. At this point, attach two pieces of the three-piece pin finding—the clasp and the joint—but wait until after firing to clamp the pin into the joint. (Unlike the silver clasp and joint, the pin is nickel and would soften during firing.) Place the clasp and joint a third of the way down the piece, and cement them on with syringe clay or thick slip. Be sure to position them the correct distance apart for the length of the pin.

15. After the piece is dry, place it faceup on strips of kiln blanket, positioned to support the joint and allow the pin findings to hang down. Follow the instructions for Firing with Stones on page 22.

16. Polish and oxidize the fired piece.

**TIP:** If you prefer, you can epoxy a one-piece pinback onto the fired piece, rather than firing separate findings in place as outlined in step 14. Attach this finding last, when all oxidizing and polishing is complete.

# Gathering Inspiration

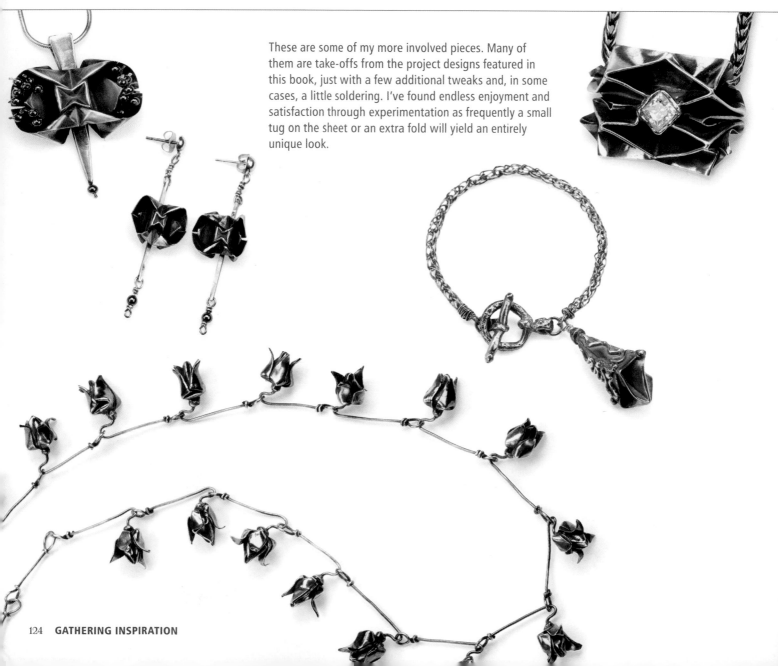

These are some of my more involved pieces. Many of them are take-offs from the project designs featured in this book, just with a few additional tweaks and, in some cases, a little soldering. I've found endless enjoyment and satisfaction through experimentation as frequently a small tug on the sheet or an extra fold will yield an entirely unique look.

# About the Author

Sara Jayne Cole has two creative passions; one is working with metal and the other is folding origami. With metal clay sheet, she has been able to join the two with dynamic success to create lyrical shapes that are components for her jewelry. Sara Jayne is a graduate silversmith and has been working with metal clay since 2000. A member of the PMC Guild and the Art Clay Society, she is a certified instructor in both PMC and Art Clay Silver. She is also an origami folder and member of Origami USA. Sara Jayne and her husband, Phil, live in Waterloo, Iowa, where she maintains a jewelry studio and teaches in the local art center. Her other interests include camping, hiking, birding, and compiling family stories for her children and grandchildren.

# Acknowledgments

I would like to thank the authors of the many origami books that taught me folding. Many thanks to all my metal clay friends who encouraged me to continue folding metal clay as my artistic statement. I should like to thank Marthe Le Van of Lark Books for suggesting I write a book and the fantastic staff at Lark Books: my editor, Linda Kopp, who is a great organizer; my project editor, Carol Taylor, who carefully folded each project from my instructions; Amanda Carestio who helped in every way; photographer Stewart O'Shields who can make the mundane into a glamour shot; illustrator Orrin Lundgren; my art director Kristi Pfeffer; and the many others who made this beautiful book possible.

Special thanks to my husband, Phil Cole, who is my best friend. I also want to thank my extended family—all of you contributed by proudly wearing my creations.

# Index

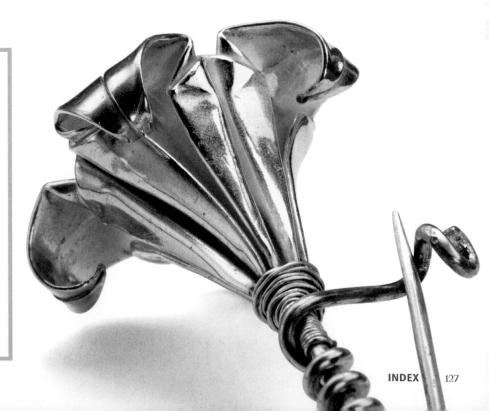

It's all on www.larkbooks.com

**Can't find the materials you need to create a project?**
Search our database for craft suppliers & sources for hard-to-find materials.

**Got an idea for a book?**
Read our book proposal guidelines and contact us.

**Want to show off your work?**
Browse current calls for entries.

**Want to know what new and exciting books we're working on?**
Sign up for our free e-newsletter.

**Feeling crafty?**
Find free, downloadable project directions on the site.

**Interested in learning more about the authors, designers & editors who create Lark books?**

# Here Are Some Other Lark Titles You May Enjoy

Available at Barnes & Noble and other booksellers everywhere

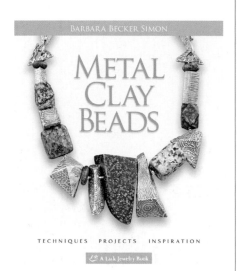

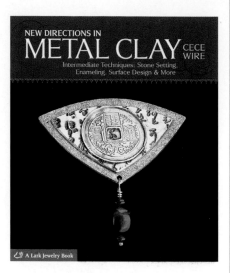

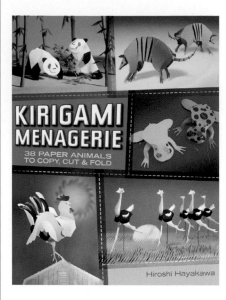

## Metal Clay Beads
Techniques, Projects, Inspiration

**by Barbara Becker Simon**

Whether you want to experiment with metal clay for the first time or have some experience and want to develop your skills, look no further than this book. In this unique, comprehensive reference, Barbara Becker Simon treats readers to 22 outstanding metal clay bead projects. An introductory section guides them through all the fundamentals, from forming and joining the clay to firing and finishing. Learn how to add gemstones, glass, and other objects; use molded and carved texture plates; etch photos into a surface; develop rich patinas; and more.

ISBN 978-1600590252

## New Directions in Metal Clay
Intermediate Techniques: Stone Setting, Enameling, Surface Design & More

**by CeCe Wire**

Beginning and experienced jewelry makers alike have embraced metal clay for its versatility and ease of use. CeCe Wire, a leader in the field, describes the fundamentals while also presenting an assortment of spectacular projects. She includes every form and formula, plus an extensive array of cutting-edge techniques that range from stone-setting to surface finishing. Numerous color photos showcase diverse possibilities, including enameling methods such as champlevé, inlaying with epoxy resin, and silk screening.

ISBN 978-1600595462

## Kirigami Menagerie
38 Paper Animals to Copy, Cut & Fold

**by Hiroshi Hayakawa**

In origami, a flat piece of paper is folded to create a dimensional object. Similarly, in traditional Japanese kirigami, paper is folded, cut, and unfolded to reveal complex patterns—like a paper snowflake. In this book Hiroshi Hayakawa has ingeniously combined these two techniques to create a charming menagerie of 38 animals, from flocks of sheep and swirling dragons to stampeding ostriches and pandas in a bamboo grove.

Full-size templates are provided to photocopy onto the card stock of your choice.

ISBN 978-1600593185